PRESENTATION
HELL

PRESENTATION
HELL

From Painful Presentations to
BETTER STORIES

**JAMES ONTRA and
ALEXANNDRA ONTRA**

LIONCREST
PUBLISHING

PRESENTATION HELL
From Painful Presentations to Better Stories

ISBN   978-1-5445-3395-7 *Hardcover*
       978-1-5445-3394-0 *Paperback*
       978-1-5445-3393-3 *Ebook*

CONTENTS

Brokenhearted   Garbage Communication   Dead End

Frustration   Conquering Fear   Harmony

Organized Slide Content   Your Corporate Story   Better Presenting

Presentations Are a Mess   Clean'm Up   Structured Story

Favors User   Favors Enterprise   Balance = Success

Media of Communication   Why No Presentations   Presentation Value

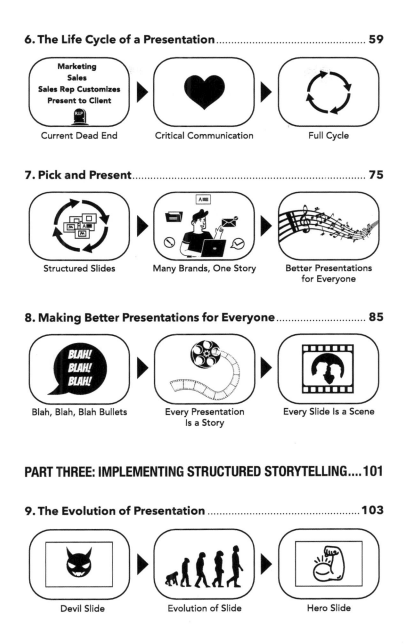

Current Dead End   Critical Communication   Full Cycle

Structured Slides   Many Brands, One Story   Better Presentations for Everyone

Blah, Blah, Blah Bullets   Every Presentation Is a Story   Every Slide Is a Scene

Devil Slide   Evolution of Slide   Hero Slide

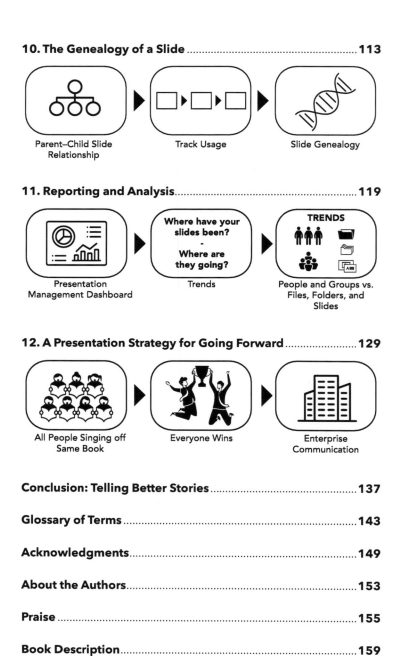

FOREWORD

THE VERY FIRST TABLE OF CONTENTS EVER CREATED IS attributed to an ancient Latin poet named Quintus Valerius Soranus, who wanted to give readers an easy way to navigate the contents of his lengthy book.[1] By the time Johannes Gutenberg invented his movable-type printing press in 1440 and began mass-producing books, it became standard practice to organize books around a table of contents.

It was a communication strategy that made it easier for readers to understand and easily access the information contained within. Instead of simply thrusting an enormous volume at someone and expecting them to make sense of it, the publisher could provide a clear and orderly structure of the contents to help readers wrap their heads around the story the author wanted to tell.

---

1 Henderson, John. 2002. "Knowing Someone through Their Books: Pliny on Uncle Pliny ('Epistles' 3.5)." *Classical Philology* 97 (3): 275. https://doi. org/10.1086/449587.

You are about to discover another revolutionary communication strategy. It's called *Structured Storytelling*, and it gives you a more powerful way to create and share presentations. In fact, the table of contents in this very book is organized as a presentation using Structured Storytelling so you can quickly grasp the information shared in the upcoming chapters in a way that is visually interesting and compelling.

It's a perfect example of what you're going to do with your presentations, transforming them into a structured story that is far more impactful than your old boring slideshows.

Let's be frank: presentations can be hell. Most of the time, they're a pain to put together, a nerve-racking experience to share, and incredibly boring to sit through. The good news is, they don't have to be that way.

James and Alex have come up with an approach that transforms presentations into compelling brand stories, an approach that gives you a way to organize all of your slide content so your entire global operation is telling the same story consistently across the board.

It's a revolutionary strategy that is going to change the way you present to clients, customers, and your own teams. And the story of Structured Storytelling begins as soon as you turn the page.

INTRODUCTION

I GOT DUMPED VIA POWERPOINT.

The year was 2005, and we'd been seeing each other for a while. To be honest, I thought the relationship was going well. We'd had some fun times, and it looked like we had a future together. Then he called me one morning and said, "Sweetheart, I'd like to meet with you and talk."

I could tell by the tone of his voice that something was wrong. "Can't we discuss it over the phone?" I asked.

"No, this needs to be done in person," he said.

Despite my misgivings, we met in the back room of a local coffee shop. The lights were dim; the place smelled like espresso. Although I could hear a few people chatting quietly, we had the back room all to ourselves.

"What's this about?" I asked.

He'd brought his laptop, and he placed it on a table as I sat down.

"I've come to a decision," he said, "and I just need to explain myself."

As I sat there, stunned, he opened PowerPoint, angled the laptop screen where I could see it clearly, and turned up the brightness.

"Wait a second," I said. "Are you about to show me a slide presentation?"

But he didn't answer. Whatever was about to happen, it clearly wasn't intended to be a two-way conversation. My boyfriend took up a position beside the laptop, a wireless clicker in his hand, and cleared his throat. Then he proceeded to walk me slide by slide through a presentation he'd created. The first slide declared his intention: *Reasons Why We Have to Break Up*. It included a nice, animated GIF of a heart cracking down the middle.

"I'm sorry, Alex, but I think our relationship is doomed," he said in a stilted voice that suggested he'd prepared his words in advance.

Introduction

"What? Why?" I was shocked. Things had been going so well. We'd just gone to dinner and a movie the night before, and we were planning to visit his parents in a few days. "Why do we *have* to break up?"

His answer was all in the presentation. The second slide was a chart showing the differences in our travel preferences. He liked camping and trekking through the wilderness, while I liked staying in nice hotels. The third slide showed our educational differences. I went to UT Austin; he went to a technical college. The fourth slide showed the differences in our entertainment preferences. Then our philosophies about money. Then our family backgrounds. And so on.

Through a series of graphs, charts, and pithy quotes from famous people, he made his case that our lives weren't aligned. It was a well-constructed argument, and the slides looked nice. Still, I wanted to refute much of what he said. Some of his points were off. However, the linear nature of the presentation wasn't conducive to a discussion, so I sat there in shock.

After about fifteen minutes, he came to his dramatic conclusion. "We're clearly not compatible, as I have demonstrated here today. We have no choice but to end our relationship."

"There are some things I'd like to say," I told him.

"I'm sorry. It was all in the presentation," he replied as he closed his laptop. "I can send you the slide deck if you want to look at it again on your own time."

And that was the end of both our coffee-shop meeting and our relationship. After he walked out, I sat there for a few minutes, nursing a cold latte and feeling a bit overwhelmed. His presentation had been mostly a one-sided information dump, and I was still processing my thoughts long after he was gone.

When I finally trudged out of the coffee shop that day, feeling hurt, frustrated, and embarrassed by the whole thing, I was a single woman again. My boyfriend had dumped me by PowerPoint.

That whole bizarre experience got me thinking about how ubiquitous slide presentations have become. It's clear why my tech-minded boyfriend broke up with me that way—a typical slideshow is a crutch for communication. It forces the discussion to move in a specific direction as you progress from slide to slide, and it has a preordained ending that can't be changed. Instead of a conversational mutual exploration of thoughts and feelings, it pushes both speaker and listener down a linear path that feels unnatural but guides them to an obligatory conclusion.

But what if things had gone differently that day? What if, instead of being forced down a linear path, I'd been able to pull out my phone and bring up pictures from all of the fun times we'd had together—our smiling faces at dinner, our smiling faces on vacation, family holidays, spending time with mutual friends?

What if I'd been able to counteract all of his charts and graphs with a series of photos and videos that told a much more poignant story? Instead of a linear, predefined presentation, that meeting in the coffee shop would have been a conversation full of genuine emotion and honest responses. It might even have salvaged the relationship. We'll never know because that conversation never happened.

As strange as that meeting sounds, it's not all that different from what takes place in the business world every day. Think about all of the dry, linear, predetermined presentations you've sat through. Think about how many of those presentations you've given yourself.

What if they were more dynamic, responsive, and impactful, drawn from a library of slides on the spot to address questions and concerns? What if, instead of trying to cobble together a brand-new presentation every time you wanted to make a sales pitch, you could draw from a preexisting wealth of content that you knew was high quality, compliant, conversational, and consistent with your brand?

It would certainly mitigate the awkwardness we all feel when giving presentations—not to mention the awkwardness we feel when listening to them.

WHO'S AFRAID OF THE BIG BAD PRESENTATION?

If you're like most people, you're probably afraid of giving presentations. There's something uncomfortable about them, isn't there? When you're building your slide deck, you can't know how your audience is going to respond, what questions they're going to ask, or how they might react to individual slides, but you still have to preordain the ending and construct a slide-by-slide path for getting them there, whether they like it or not.

Despite the obvious deficiencies, presentations have become ubiquitous in the modern world. They're everywhere. Think about how many hours of your life you've spent cobbling together slide decks for sales pitches, conferences, and board meetings. Think about the time you've spent pulling together graphics, statistics, and quotes from disparate sources, hunting through folders, trying to anticipate your audience. On average, a person spends about five hours preparing a presentation. All for what? Just to give a thirty-minute presentation that feels unnatural.

But what if you could pull from a corporate slide library that had individual slides for every issue: who you are, what you do, how you do it, why you do it. What if you could read and react to your clients' needs on the fly with valued documentation? Imagine this:

A few minutes before giving a presentation, you realize you need an emotional video to confirm what you're talking about. Fortunately, you already have the perfect videos in your slide library that you can pull up right now. You also need some statistical data to back up your claims. A nice chart is readily available in your slide library as well.

> What if you could read and react to your clients' needs on the fly with valued documentation?

More than that, imagine if every single video, picture, chart, PDF, and spreadsheet in your library was already formatted and ready to present as a slide, and the language was consistent across all of them. Think about how that would boost your credibility and ability to respond to your audience in real time.

We call this *Presentation Management*, and we are convinced it's the future of presentations.

In this book, we're going to provide you with a methodology for implementing Presentation Management in your company through *Structured Storytelling*. You'll learn how to clean up the vast, tangled mess of slides throughout your company and create an organized slide library that enables every single team member to communicate more effectively.

With Structured Storytelling, you will save a ton of time by reusing all of your assets, and you will have data about which slides are being used—when, where, and by whom. You will know which slides are most effective, so you can constantly tweak the content to make every slide better and better for your entire organization. And you'll be able to follow conversations, respond at critical moments, and reinforce your message, greatly increasing your chances of achieving a mutually beneficial ending.

That's the power of Structured Storytelling.

OUR ROAD TO STRUCTURED STORYTELLING

We are James Ontra and AlexAnndra Ontra, a brother-sister team with over thirty years of experience helping clients tell their stories more effectively. Through our career from iXL Pitchman to Iguana Interactive and Ontra Presentations and Shufflrr, we've worked with numerous global corporations across a broad array of industries, including

Introduction

ABC, NBC, CBS, FOX, Warner Bros., Disney, ESPN, Comedy Central, AOL, NFL, NBA, Hilton, Starbucks, Choice Hotels, US Bank, Comerica, and several global pharmaceutical companies—to name just a few.

Our road to Structured Storytelling began in 1993 when James helped create one of the world's first interactive catalogs, Miramar CD-I, which gave clients an interactive presentation kiosk. Targeted specifically to furniture manufacturers, the technology was ahead of its time, and business leaders shied away from it.

However, in 1998, as head of business development for Micro Interactive, James began promoting and selling the first interactive multimedia presentation system, Micro Interactive's Iguana, which provided users with a multimedia library they could use for presentations. Among its early adopters were IBM, NBC Olympics, Lucent Technologies, British Airways, Cigna, Hilton Hotels, and MGM's James Bond franchise. Later, the company became iXL and the system's name was changed to Pitchman.

In 2000, James raised venture capital and spun out the Pitchman laptop presentation division of iXL, becoming CEO of the new company, Iguana Interactive. His sister, AlexAnndra, left her exciting job in advertising to join him, and the dynamic brother-sister duo was born. We soon found ourselves working with the NBA, the NFL, American Express, and many others. Unfortunately, Iguana

Interactive didn't last long. Our offices were at 14 Wall Street, just blocks from the World Trade Center, and after 9/11, investors pulled out, and the company went bust.

However, from the ashes of Iguana, we started Ontra Presentations, with only a borrowed desk, a phone, and a license to Iguana Interactive's software. After ninety days of grueling cold calls, we landed our first clients: ABC National Television Sales, and then our second, Towers Perrin. From there, we landed many more high-profile clients, including a number of Fortune-level companies.

When YouTube came along it 2005, it changed the presentation game by democratizing digital video. Suddenly, clients were no longer willing to pay a premium for video and animations in their presentations, even if the quality was better. Our business model was falling out of favor, but a client said to us, "Can't you just make the video work in PowerPoint?" We listened and went to work developing the PPTshare Slide Library for PowerPoint, a desktop slide library that connected to a central network and enabled users to drag videos into their presentations.

And now, after working with hundreds of clients and developing multiple software solutions, we're using everything we've learned over more than fifty years combined of Presentation Management experience to refine a strategy, process, and technology that enables companies to implement structured stories. As part of that mission, we've created Shufflrr, an elegant, easy solution that ensures brand and message compliance, while giving your team a quick way to create and share presentations. More than that, we work with clients every day to help them transform their linear presentations into dynamic and responsive conversations that tell a story and respond on the fly to audience needs.

But is this kind of Presentation Management approach even necessary? Does the world really need Structured Storytelling? We think so, and we'd like to make our case. To do that, we'll go all the way back to 1948.

AN OVERLOOKED CATEGORY OF COMMUNICATION

David Ogilvy, the so-called "Father of Advertising," founded his agency Ogilvy & Mather in 1948 upon a singular promise to corporate leaders, which said, in essence, "If you give me all of your advertising, marketing, and sales dollars, I will use research and focus on different categories of communication to achieve better creativity, better planning, and better placement for better results. In turn, you will be able to sell more widgets."

The media of communication that Ogilvy identified as key were print, radio, billboards, and television. Much later, you can add digital to that equation, for a total of five key categories of communication. Multibillion-dollar marketing and sales industries have sprung up around each of them.

But do you notice one very popular category of communication missing from that list?

Despite being ubiquitous in the world today, *presentations* are a medium of communication that lacks its own industry. This is despite the fact that slides have been around since the beginning of human civilization. What were the paintings on cave walls if not an early version of PowerPoint slides that tribal leaders could use to tell the tribe's important stories? What were the stained-glass windows in medieval cathedrals but slides that could be used to tell the religion's stories to mostly illiterate people?

Every single university lecture hall is built around giving presentations, with slides as a critical component of most professors' teaching styles. Salespeople use presentations all of the time when they're in front of clients. Yet the same company that will spend tens of millions of dollars on a Super Bowl ad will then send a salesperson to talk to a potential customer they met through that ad, and that salesperson will use a presentation that they hastily put together the night before.

Presentations are everywhere because the technology exists to present almost anywhere at any time. It's a whole category of communication that people rely on every day, so isn't it time we started devoting energy and resources to making presentations more powerful and effective? Imagine taking your tangled mess of slides and transforming them into a structured slide library that enables every single person in your organization to communicate as powerfully, effectively, and responsively as your CEO.

> Imagine if every single person in your organization could communicate as powerfully, effectively, and responsively as your CEO.

In the following chapters, we're going to provide you with everything you need to know to implement Presentation Management through Structured Storytelling in your organization. You'll be able to bring together all of the slides, images, videos, charts, and content throughout your entire organization and organize them into a slide library with consistent messaging that will transform every presentation into a more dynamic, impactful conversation where every presentation tells a story, and every slide is a scene.

category of communication that people rely on every day, so isn't it time we started devoting energy and resources to making presentations more powerful and effective? Imagine taking your tangled mess of slides and transforming them into a structured slide library that enables every single person in your organization to communicate as powerfully, effectively, and responsively as your CEO.

> Imagine if every single person in your organization could communicate as powerfully, effectively, and responsively as your CEO.

In the following chapters, we're going to provide you with everything you need to know to implement Presentation Management through Structured Storytelling in your organization. You'll be able to bring together all of the slides, images, videos, charts, and content throughout your entire organization and organize them into a slide library with consistent messaging that will transform every presentation into a more dynamic, impactful conversation where every presentation tells a story, and every slide is a scene.

PART 1

STRUCTURED STORYTELLING

CHAPTER 1

WHY ARE PRESENTATIONS SO HARD?

You've no doubt felt the perfect storm of fears that hit hard when you have to give a presentation. There's nothing quite like it. Still, I was even more nervous than usual on this particular occasion.

It was early in my career, before I joined my brother, when I still worked in advertising. I was supposed to give a big pitch to Loews Hotels, an exclusive luxury hotel brand in North America. This was a huge opportunity for the ad agency I worked for, but it was an even bigger opportunity for me and my career.

I couldn't afford to get it wrong, so I worked on my presentation all week. I wrote, rewrote, and refined the script, then I practiced it over and over in front of the mirror and in front of my roommates. Putting together the slide deck took many hours as I hunted down files, pictures, statistics, and charts, then designed and redesigned each slide. I desperately wanted everything to be just right.

By the time the conference rolled around on Monday morning, I had practiced the presentation so many times that I had every word and inflection memorized. The slides were as good as I could get them, and I was as ready as I could be.

Then I walked into the conference room and saw the hotel executives sitting there, along with my boss and my creative director. I saw the big podium in the front of the room, the projector on the table, and all of the confidence I'd built up over the weekend just evaporated. There was a lot riding on this presentation, and the pressure was intense. How in the world had I ever imagined I could pull this off?

When it was my turn to speak, I walked to the podium like I was walking the last mile on Death Row. The first slide was on the screen, and all of the hotel executives were staring at me. I had the clicker in my right hand, my left hand pressing the printed copy of my script to the podium. And I just froze. Even though my script was right there in front of me, I couldn't get the words out.

I really wanted to impress these guys, but my heart was pounding, I was sweating, and the words just wouldn't come. As I struggled, I suddenly developed a searing anxiety-induced headache. Awkward seconds passed as I tried to somehow collect my thoughts and press on, but the headache was getting more intense. My worst-case scenario had come true.

Fortunately, the creative director realized something was very wrong. Hopping up from his seat, he came to the podium and leaned in close.

"Are you okay, AlexAnndra?" he asked quietly.

"Um," I stuttered. And he just took over. Massaging my temples, I stumbled to the table and sat down, and the creative director took over my presentation. He made the pitch and saved the meeting, but I felt humiliated. I'd ruined my big chance to impress both the client and my boss. All of my hard work and preparations had been for nothing.

Later, the client gave the following feedback: "We like Alex, but she's a little too junior." Ouch! And all because I blew my ten-minute part of a presentation.

Even if you've never had an experience quite so dramatic, you can surely relate to the fear we feel when giving presentations. There's usually a tremendous amount of pressure, especially in a sales presentation where a large amount of money might be riding on a single pitch. Hell, your whole career might be riding on it.

Our fear of public speaking and presentations isn't merely anecdotal. According to the National Institute of Mental Health, 75 percent of people rank public speaking as their number one fear, even above death.[2] It sounds extreme, but it's understandable. That day when I froze during my presentation, it kind of felt like a brush with death—career death, if nothing else.

There's even a word for it: *glossophobia.* According to Dr. Timothy J. Legg, in an article on *Healthline,* "When faced with having to give a presentation, many people experience the classic fight-or-flight response. This is the body's way of preparing to defend itself against perceived threats." He lists the common symptoms of this fight-or-flight response as rapid heartbeat, trembling, sweating, nausea or vomiting, shortness of breath or hyperventilating, dizziness, muscle tension, and an urge to get away.[3] How many of these symptoms have you experienced? Personally, we've experienced almost all of them at one time or another.

Add in a slide deck, and suddenly the fear is compounded. It's no longer just about getting the words right, sounding confident and compelling, because you also have to make

---

2 Pat Ladouceur, "What We Fear More than Death - Information on Anxiety and Other Anxiety Related Mental Health Disorders," MentalHelp.net, February 2017, https://www.mentalhelp.net/blogs/what-we-fear-more-than-death.

3 Susan Y. Morris, "Overcoming Glossophobia: Causes, Treatment, and More," Healthline, November 23, 2016, https://www.healthline.com/health/glossophobia#symptoms.

sure your slide deck is well-designed, communicates your ideas clearly, and builds your case well from slide to slide. That's fear upon fear. While lots of preparation usually helps, somehow it just can't take away the terrible anxiety we all feel when we finally stand up and approach the podium with clicker in hand.

THE PERFECT STORM OF FEARS

When you think about it, presentations really are a perfect storm of fears. There's the fear of failure. There's the fear of judgment. There's also the fear that occurs during slide preparation when you're trying to anticipate the questions that your audience might ask. Despite your best efforts, you just never know what's going to happen during the meeting. Since you're putting together a linear presentation, somehow you must try to anticipate any issues that might come up, so you can respond to them. At the same time, you simply can't anticipate *everything*, and you know it.

There's also fear of deadlines and any other time constraints you might be facing. You might be trying to cram a whole encyclopedia's worth of information about a product or service into a twenty-minute presentation. Finally, there's the uniquely horrible fear that comes from stage fright, which can produce a whole range of physiological side effects: sweating, stammering, hands shaking, crying, headache, and so much more.

No wonder presentations are so hard. It takes such a long time to put together your slides and make them look good enough to present to a client. Then, as if that weren't challenging enough, you have to stand in front of a room of people and talk through those slides one by one, fingers crossed that someone doesn't ask a question you didn't anticipate. A lucrative deal might be on the line. Your job might be on the line. Your income could be at stake. The success or even the very survival of your company might be riding on a single presentation. Even if none of those things are true, there's the simple fact that no one wants to look stupid or incompetent.

Furthermore, there's a vast gulf between a *great* presentation and an *okay* presentation just like there's a huge difference between winning a gold medal and winning a silver medal in the Olympics. Gold-medal winners do the talkshow circuit, appear in commercials, and make graduation speeches at colleges. You can probably name some gold-medal winners of past Olympics off the top of your head. Silver-medal winners are mostly forgotten.

People remember amazing presentations. They remember the people who gave them. Merely okay presentations disappear into the fog of time. It's the same with movies. Everyone knows the names of the masters of cinema, people like Steven Spielberg and Christopher Nolan, directors who make powerful, landmark films. Almost nobody knows the name of a director who churns out decent-but-not-amazing action movies or mediocre romantic comedies.

> There's a vast gulf between a great presentation and an *okay* presentation. People remember amazing presentations. Merely okay presentations disappear into the fog of time.

So it's not enough to just survive a presentation without embarrassing yourself. Somehow, you have to amaze your audience. And just like the masters of cinema, if you really want to "wow" people, you have to get all the nuances of a presentation just right. Why is someone like Spielberg considered a great director, while so many other filmmakers are consigned to obscurity?

Because of the consistent quality of his movies, where each scene is carefully considered in the overall flow of telling a compelling story. He's good at storytelling. He knows how to use the medium of motion pictures to tell a good story from beginning to end. The same goes for presentations. In her book *Resonate,* Nancy Duarte talks about the importance of using story in presentations to inform, inspire, and persuade audiences. As she put it in an interview, "The greatest communicators have unknowingly used a story pattern. They not only use anecdotes effectively, but their communication followed a persuasive story pattern of tension and release."[4]

---

4 Bob Morris, "Nancy Duarte: An Interview by Bob Morris," Blogging on Business, June 7, 2011, https://bobmorris.biz/nancy-duarte-an-interview-by-bob-morris.

To create a good presentation, you have to think about the overarching story, the total production, and the role that every element plays. Even then, it's hard to tell if your presentations are getting better. You either land the sale or you don't, but there's no box office to track your success, no professional presentation critics to tell you that you're mastering the art, no gold or silver medals for presentations, so you're forever insecure.

A SOLUTION FOR EVERY FEAR

We believe Structured Storytelling is the solution to this perfect storm of fears. Structured Storytelling is an essential part of Presentation Management, and it's sorely lacking in most businesses. It's the difference between a messy room, where everything is just strewn about in no particular order, and an organized room, where you know the place and purpose of everything.

Think of it this way. If your bedroom looks like something from an episode of *Hoarders*, it's a lot harder to dress nicely for a formal event, because you find yourself digging through drawers and piles looking for each item that you need. On the other hand, if your room is tidy, everything well organized and put in its place, then it's no problem at all. Shirts are hanging over here, pants and jackets over there. Shoes are on a rack in the corner, socks in the top dresser drawer.

"Oh, I need my blue hat? No problem. I know exactly where it is. And that matching tie? I know where that is, as well, and it's ready to go."

It's not a perfect analogy, but that's a bit like what Presentation Management does for you. That messy closet is like your network, with all of your presentation files dumped haphazardly in folders on various hard drives. File names might not be consistent. There's little organization. Your organization is full of "slide hoarders" who have created a big mess of graphics, spreadsheets, slides, PDFs, and more, so it's really hard to find what you need when you need it.

But Presentation Management imposes structure and order to all of those files. Your files and content become well organized, and you can grab what you want when you want it, even if you suddenly have to find something with no warning.

When you practice good Presentation Management, your presentations become more conversational because you can follow, adjust, and respond to your audience on the fly. All of your content is tidy and well placed. It's easier to access exactly what you want when you want it. It's also easier to give your presentation a good, strong structure because you have access to a Structured Storytelling library where all messaging is clear, consistent, and readily available.

It certainly would have made AlexAnndra's presentation to Loews Hotels easier, and helped her overcome her fear of public speaking, if she'd had a vast library of content at her fingertips for responding to any questions or concerns. Instead, she had a single linear presentation upon which the weight of a large, lucrative deal rested. Not to mention the actual physical response: a searing anxiety-induced headache.

What if, instead of being a speech presented from a podium in the corner, with a series of unchangeable slides that had to be worked through to reach a final concluding "yea or nay" moment, it had been a relational, reactive conversation with a comfortable back-and-forth? And instead of a preordained ending, it had been a mutually beneficial discussion that was able to take the audience where they wanted to go with readily available information already formatted to present? It certainly would have put her mind at ease. Being conversational does more to build real relationships. It's friendly, intimate, and lacks artificiality.

What happens with a linear presentation when someone in the audience asks a question that you weren't prepared for? Typically, you have to respond with, "I'll get back to you about that. I don't have that information with me right now." That fear of unanticipated questions is one of the biggest contributing factors to presentation anxiety and glossophobia.

What if you could respond to any and every question on the fly with confidence? "Oh, I have a slide about that right here! Just a second."

And furthermore, what if this conversational aspect of presentations didn't have to come at the expense of constructing a powerful and compelling slide deck that tells a clear, consistent story from beginning to end just like a really good Steven Spielberg movie? What if every slide you pulled from your slide library was a well-constructed scene helping to tell your overarching brand story?

Presentation Management gives you all of this. Can you see how it eliminates much of the fear that we all feel about giving presentations? Key to its effectiveness is what we call *Structured Storytelling*. Let's look a little closer at what Structured Storytelling is and how it works.

CHAPTER 2

WHAT IS STRUCTURED STORYTELLING?

SCRIPPS NETWORKS WAS AN AMERICAN MASS MEDIA company formed in 2008 that owned a wide variety of niche cable TV channels. In 2018, they merged with Discovery Communications, adding dozens of media properties to their portfolio, and in 2022, Discovery acquired Warner-Media to create Warner Bros. Discovery with hundreds of media properties. When we worked with them fifteen years ago, their list of niche channels included HGTV, Great American Country, Food Network, Travel Channel, Fine Living, and many more.

The challenge they faced then was that the company had to somehow sell their suite of seemingly disparate channels to advertisers all across the country. How could a single company with so many different channels targeting so many different niche audiences possibly present them all together into a unified whole so that they could effectively pitch them? It had the potential to be the most scattered, messy, and boring presentation ever made, not because there was anything wrong with the company but simply because there was just so much information to present and no apparent way to tie it all together.

A young sales leader at the company named Jon Steinlauf came up with a brilliant solution: he decided to use Structured Storytelling. His marketing team created a fictional, idealized household to represent the audience for the family of channels. Then a story was created around the lives of each member of that family, with each of the company's networks representing a different component of the family's lives. Nancy Duarte discusses this strategy in her book *Resonate*. The slides were designed as scenes, each one telling the story of one of their networks, and then we used Ontra Presentation software to structure the slides for easy playback.

That story went something like this:

"Scripps channels touch every aspect of life for your typical American family. Oh, you have to make something for dinner to feed your family after a long day at work? Here's the Food Network. Now, it's the weekend, and you want to relax by doing some gardening in the backyard? Here's HGTV. Also, you have a week of vacation coming up, and you want to take your spouse somewhere romantic? Here's the Travel Channel."

This story became a compelling presentation that tied all of the channels together into an overarching tale for the parent company's target audience—the ideal family—that they were able to use in a high-end roadshow to sell their programming across the country. The presentation was so well structured and such an effective story that media planners could take and present it to specific clients to sell ad time.

Additionally, that structured story was created to be flexible, so it could be used in a variety of different sales scenarios, from the high-profile upfront roadshow with C-suite executives and talent to the one-on-one meetings between account executives and media planners. Account executives could customize the presentation as needed in order to get a contract.

In the end, using Structured Storytelling was a brilliant approach that won Jon acclaim and propelled him to the top of his career. He became Vice President of Ad Sales at Scripps, and he's now Chief US Advertising Sales Officer at Discovery. If you can tell a good and compelling story, you become more effective at sales, and anyone who can consistently deliver profits is going to reap the rewards in their career. It's as simple as that.

"[Structured Storytelling] allows all of our salespeople to speak intelligently whether talking about the details of one program or the value of working with Scripps in general. With [Structured Storytelling], they can now cross-sell the networks, which translates into higher revenues for all of Scripps."

—Jon Steinlauf, SVP of Ad Sales, Scripps Networks (current: Board Member and Chief US Advertising Sales Officer for Warner Bros. Discovery)

When you structure your presentation to tell an overarching story about your company, where each component of your company fits neatly into that story, then the value of what you have to offer becomes clear. Suddenly, anyone can understand who you are, what you do, why you do it, and most importantly, why it matters. The institution as a whole can be sold on a higher value than the sum of its individual parts.

That's the real power of Structured Storytelling. The message is always on point, and every slide points toward the same horizon, which is the ultimate thesis of your entire company.

With Structured Storytelling, your message is always on point, and every slide points toward the same horizon.

IMAGINE THE POSSIBILITIES

Imagine having the ability to quickly pull the most relevant slides and knowing that any slide you pull from your library will already be formatted to present, consistent in its messaging, and easy to fit into the story you're trying to tell. Several years ago, Scripps participated in an upfront presentation for Ford executives in Detroit. Like any upfront, it was essentially a large sales presentation to determine how ad money was going to be allocated among various agencies.

Just before the big meeting, a Ford executive for their truck division approached the Scripps account manager and said, "Hey, would it be possible to give a quick pitch specifically for our truck division?"

With the old linear presentations, this would have been an unreasonable request. The account manager had almost no prep time to put together a brand-new presentation with a different focus. However, he merely smiled and said, "Sure, no problem."

Since he used our Structured Storytelling system, he was able to quickly pull the five most relevant slides from his library. They were already on message and formatted to present, so within minutes, he was ready to deliver a poignant pitch to the truck division that fit into the overall company message.

Can you see how radically this changes the game?

In his book *Enablement Mastery*, Elay Cohen tells a story about attending an executive meeting at the Salesforce office in San Francisco to discuss their latest corporate pitch presentation. Marc Benioff, the CEO of Salesforce, brought the heads of product marketing, corporate communications, and sales to the meeting, and then he went through their presentation one slide at a time, carefully explaining the purpose of each one using customer examples and an overall story arc.

Elay then writes: "The energy was engaging and tense. Everyone wanted to win. That was the culture. It was the ultimate in messaging alignment...He wanted every sales and customer-facing employee to practice and deliver the corporate pitch in front of a person who would sign off that they had delivered the presentation on message and according to expectations."

While they weren't using Structured Storytelling, the idea of ensuring that every slide is on message and meets expectations fits right into the Structured Storytelling approach—every slide used by every salesperson in front of every client has a consistent message and fits in perfectly with the company's story.

Imagine you're a junior executive facing an incredibly important sales presentation with a huge potential client the very next day. A lot of money is at stake, not to mention your standing in the company and your future career path. Normally, you'd be terrified of falling flat on your face and blowing the whole deal. You'd feel that same perfect storm of fears that AlexAnndra felt when presenting to the Loews Hotels executives.

But what if you knew you already had the tools at your fingertips to give a clear, compelling presentation? And what if those tools worked like a continual education system that only got better, and made *you* better, every time you gave a presentation? What if a whole library of slides was at your fingertips, and you knew every slide was already signed off on and getting tweaked and improved over time to stay on message?

Think about how much better communication would be throughout your entire organization. Think about how much more effective it was for Jon at Scripps to try to sell their suite of channels when they were able to tell a compelling story about their company in which every channel played a clear role in the lives of their target audience.

Structured Storytelling transforms your tangled mess of slides into a storytelling library. It works a bit like the photo album on your smartphone. If you have a smartphone handy, go ahead and open your Photos app right now. What do you see? Typically, you see a screen that says "My Albums," in which all of your media files have already been subdivided into thematic groupings for you. Maybe there's one that says "Favorites," "People," "Locations," "Camping Trip," another that says "Birthday," or "Work Photos," and so on.

If you scroll down, there are also folders that contain photos and videos of specific people, then links for specific types of media. Every picture or video you've taken on your iPhone is readily available, automatically sorted into thematic folders, and ready to be presented.

Suppose you run into a friend at the grocery store one afternoon, and she says, "Hey, how was your trip to Disney World last week? I'll bet it was a lot of fun."

All you have to do is open your Photos app and open the "Disney World" folder. Suddenly, without any preparation time, you have a whole bunch of pictures and videos to help you answer that question. You don't show your friend every picture, of course. Instead, you choose the ones that you think will be most interesting and highlight the story that you want to tell about your vacation.

"Here's the hotel where we stayed," you say, tapping a relevant photo to bring it up on the screen. Then you tap another photo. "And this was our favorite restaurant. You can see how amazing the food was in this picture right here."

"It looks like you had a great time," your friend replies. "Did your kids have a favorite ride in the theme parks?"

"They sure did," you say. "They really liked Dumbo the Flying Elephant. Here's a short video of the kids on the ride. Take a look."

"Wow, it looks really fun," your friend says. "It really makes me want to take my family there, too."

Every picture or video you bring up is relevant to the overall story, which enables you to 1) tell the story of your recent vacation effectively, while at the same time 2) following the conversation with your friend in a way that feels natural.

Structured Storytelling transforms your tangled mess of slides into a storytelling library.

With Structured Storytelling, you can rest assured that every slide in every folder is on message, is consistent with every aspect of your brand, and tells a compelling story that can easily become a scene in whatever presentation you're giving. Plus, it's being constantly updated and improved. That's what we're helping you work toward. Getting there will require confronting your own tangled mess of slides, but don't worry. We're going to help you do that, too. Let's get started.

CHAPTER 3

FROM THE TANGLED MESS OF SLIDES

Our friend Scott had an opportunity to present to his company's biggest supplier, but he only had twenty-four hours to put his slide deck together. It was an incredibly important meeting that would determine the company's future relationship with the supplier, so he knew he had to do a good job. But with so little time to prepare, he didn't know where to begin.

As he sat in his office, feeling the anxiety starting to build, he remembered a presentation the previous summer that his coworker Sally had given on the same topic. It had gone so well that the audience applauded. Some of those slides were relevant to his supplier meeting, so he called Sally.

"Hey there, Sal, can you send me the slides from your presentation last summer?" he asked. "You know, the one where the client applauded afterward."

"I'll have to hunt them down," Sally replied. "I think they're on a flash drive somewhere, but I'm not sure."

"Okay, thanks," he said. "If you could get them to me sometime this evening, that would be great."

"I'm not sure if I can, but I'll do my best. I haven't touched those slides in months. They could be anywhere."

"Just do your best," Scott said, but inwardly, he was thinking, *Please, hurry up and find them, Sally. I really need those slides!*

After that, Scott spent a long time hunting through his own computer folders, looking for some other content that he needed. There was a specific case study he wanted to use, but he couldn't find it anywhere. Finally, he summoned his assistant, Bob, to see if he could help.

"We published a case study for a client in Ontario," Scott said. "I really need it for my presentation tomorrow, but I seem to have misplaced it. Do you happen to know what we did with it?"

"I'll see what I can find out," Bob replied, as he scurried off to his desk.

He returned a while later and shrugged apologetically. "Sorry, Scott, but it turns out that case study was pulled for legal review last month due to a lawsuit related to some claims we made in it. I requested a copy from legal, and they sent an automatic reply that said we would get a response in forty-eight hours."

"I don't *have* forty-eight hours," Scott replied. "The presentation is tomorrow!"

By now, he was starting to get frantic.

"I'm going to get a copy of that darn case study," he muttered, "even if I have to go over there and talk to legal in person."

Desperate, he rushed out of the office and headed across town to the building where the legal department was located. This was a career-making (or breaking) presentation; he couldn't afford to give a second-rate show. He wasn't going to let a little legal complexity get in the way!

When he finally spoke to someone in the legal department, the sheer panic in his voice seemed to help, and they released the case study that he needed. Still, there was a lot more content that he needed, and he'd already spent a couple of hours trying to pull things together.

As he drove back to his own office, he remembered a commercial that the company had run about four years earlier that really hit on the right point, so he called the video production team and begged them to track it down. They finally agreed.

In the end, after bringing together all of the disparate pieces of content, including photos, videos, slides, and charts, and finally creating the slide deck for his presentation, he looked up and realized he was the only person left in the office building. Glancing at the clock, he discovered that he'd been working on the presentation for more than five hours. Now, he just had to practice his speech a few times. He might even be able to squeeze in a couple hours of sleep, though he was so anxious, he thought a few cups of coffee would have to do.

And how did the presentation to the supplier turn out in the end? According to our friend, "It was okay, I guess."

That's a lot of fear, frustration, and frantic work just to achieve an "okay, I guess" for your most important supplier, but that's how it goes all too often in the world of presentations.

ORGANIZING THE MESS

To be completely honest, this is a somewhat fictionalized account of a real story that happened to a friend of ours, but we've all had experiences like Scott's, hunting around the network looking for content we need for a presentation. You open a folder, find a file that looks like the right one, realize it's not exactly what you wanted. Then you open another folder, find the file, but the numbers are out of date.

Then you're looking for that one specific chart. You know you've seen it before. You remember using it last year, but you've forgotten where you saved it. Eventually, you track it down to a folder on a different computer in the same network, but someone has messed with it, changing some of the information. Now, you have to change it back to make it work in your presentation.

Oh, and then there's that one video you need to use, but you can't find it anywhere. Did it get deleted? You look all over the place for it, but it's nowhere to be found. Finally, you call the ad department, and they direct you to a subfolder. There's the video you wanted. It turns out, the name of the file got changed. Also, when you open the video, you realize it's too long for your presentation. You'll have to edit it down.

As you bring all of your content together—logos, backgrounds, infographics, white papers, and more—you realize they're all out of whack. The backgrounds don't match, and some of the logos are out of date. You have to update some of the customer profile information. Now, you've got thirty different files open on your computer at the same time, and you're trying to format all of the slides, which takes forever.

"Maybe I should go and talk to the guy down the hall who's really good at making PowerPoint slides," you think. "He could probably help with all of the formatting. I'm not a graphic designer, after all. Hopefully, he's not busy right now."

By the time you're done, you've wasted far more time than you thought you would.

You can easily spend hours and hours just to prepare for a fairly short presentation, and even then, a single unanticipated response from the audience might derail the whole thing.

It's exhausting just thinking about it.

Our friend Scott eventually embraced Structured Storytelling, and it radically changed everything about his presentations for the better. Now, instead of spending more than five of his own hours, plus Bob's, Sally's, and legal's time, trying to hunt down content, put together a slide deck, and practice his speech, he says he spends about fifteen minutes!

All of the content he could possibly need is there in his library, readily accessible, easy to find, already on message and formatted to present. No more reinventing the wheel every time he has to present, no more chasing down content, driving across town, or begging people to help him, which means the anxiety and frustration have been almost entirely eliminated.

In our experience, five hours to prepare a slide deck is pretty typical, so think about all of the time that Scott has reclaimed. Let's assume he had a forty-hour workweek, and he did just one presentation a week. With Structured Storytelling, he reclaimed about 12 percent of his week, time he can now spend on more productive things.

You can get back so much lost time, money, and productivity just by giving your big mess of content an organized structure. If all of those slides were organized and readily accessible, then anyone could find what they wanted when they wanted it. Content could be reused instantly. You would no longer have dozens, hundreds, possibly thousands of people in your company putting together slide presentations on their own, telling their own versions of your corporate story.

Not only is this revolutionary for branding, but it's great from a legal and liability perspective. No one is going to be selling the wrong information to customers and putting you on the hook for things you can't deliver. No one will accidentally use a slide with the wrong price or a missing legal requirement.

> Presentation Management is revolutionary for branding, and it's great from a legal and liability perspective as well.

In Part Two of this book, we're going to walk you through a process for creating this level of organization, but for now, consider the difference it's going to make throughout your organization. A tangled mess of slides reflects poorly on any company. It conveys the sense that your company isn't managed well and can't deliver efficiently, and that has a far-reaching impact on customer satisfaction.

If someone walked into your office and saw trash piled in the corners and messy stacks of paper covering every surface, they wouldn't be excited about working with you. Yet that's exactly what presentation content is like in so many companies—a big mess—and it shows in the inconsistency and lack of quality in the presentations people are giving. Every salesperson presents the same content differently, tells different stories, and some use old logos and outdated branded content. Presenters struggle to respond to clients.

"I'll get back to you on that" is a constant refrain. All of this reflects poorly on your company as a whole.

It's time for a change. It's time to start cleaning up that mess and creating your own structured slide library. It's time to turn five hours of prep time for a presentation into fifteen minutes, so your people can focus on more productive tasks, like building client relationships.

PART 2

THE HOW-TO OF STRUCTURED STORYTELLING

CHAPTER 4

ENTERPRISE FILES
FOR EVERYDAY USE

IT'S AMAZING WHAT YOU FIND ONCE YOU BEGIN CLEANING a really messy room. As you pick through overflowing drawers, drag piles of stuff out of the closet and corners, and dig under furniture, you discover all kinds of stuff that you'd either lost or forgotten about.

"Oh, hey, I bought this pair of boots years ago! How long have they been stuffed in the back of the closet? And, wow, look at this old photo album from college! It must have fallen behind my desk when I first moved into this house. Hey, here's a bunch of old paperwork in a folder. I wonder if any of these papers are important? Whoa, a twenty-dollar bill behind this lamp!"

Cleaning and organizing a big mess is a chore, but it's exciting to discover just how much you've got tucked away. You might come across some real treasures.

"Whoa, look at this vintage leather wallet that belonged to my grandfather. I forgot I put it in this drawer. And here's a bunch of T-shirts that I thought were lost."

The experience is similar when you start putting together your library of slides. The sheer amount of content that is available on computers across your network might shock you. As the VP of sales at Brighthouse Networks put it, "We found slides we never knew we had."

Of course, there's a right way and a wrong way to clean a room. The wrong way would be to rush through it, toss a bunch of stuff in boxes, and sweep the rest under the rug. The right way means taking your time, bringing everything together, and imposing some organization going forward. As Ben Franklin said, "A place for everything, everything in its place."

So, if you have to attend a friend's wedding this weekend, you now know exactly where your best suit is located in the closet. If you want to show a visiting relative that vintage wallet, you now know it's in the top drawer of your dresser. If you need to quickly grab some athletic clothes for a tennis match, you know right where to go. You know exactly where to go to find whatever you need, and everything is clean, organized, and ready to go.

That was what Brighthouse did when they created their slide library. They didn't just throw a bunch of files into a shared folder like they were tossing junk into a bucket. Instead, they took the time to create a structure for their overarching company story, and then made sure that there was a subdivision in their library for each chapter of that story, with separate sections for each region, show, audience, and time slot.

The logical structure meant that when a team member logs into their slide library, they are following a story. And within that story, they are choosing slides that are best suited for their meeting. They can pick the slides (i.e., scenes) for their own presentation, with each scene curated to move the story along. This kind of discipline in Presentation Management on the front end saves an incredible amount of time and empowers your entire team going forward in an amazing way.

"We found slides we never knew we had."

–VP of Sales, Brighthouse Networks

You have so many assets throughout your organization, far more perhaps than you realize, with tons of relevant content parked in folders on networks, cloud storage, computers, and flash drives all over the place: case studies, product descriptions, infographics, quarterly reports, org charts, company history, messages from the CEO, videos, memes, social posts, and more. All you have to do is collect them, bring them together, and impose some structure on them.

As you begin the process of bringing all of your files together, you're going to be surprised at what you discover.

"Oh, hey, look at this marketing material I found in this folder. It's from last year, but it's still relevant. And here's a sales video from that conference in February. I've been wondering where it went. And the graphic on this flash drive is incredible. I didn't realize marketing had made it. It perfectly illustrates our onboarding process. Clients would love it. Wow, there's so much good stuff in here. I didn't know we had all of this content!"

That's the kind of thing we hear frequently when helping people build their slide libraries.

START DEALING WITH THE MESS

The first stage in creating your slide library is to find the everyday files that are located all over your network. If you're like most companies, you have a lot more relevant content buried in folders all over the place than you can possibly imagine. Think about all of the PowerPoint slide decks from past presentations that have been saved and forgotten, or the numerous pictures and videos that are just sitting in cloud storage waiting to be reused, not to mention charts, graphs, statistics, articles, case studies, white papers, and more.

The next stage is to weed through all of that content you've brought together to find the very best, weed out the duplicates, and then organize and make them available to your people for everyday use through a centralized library.

If you'll pardon an unusual metaphor, imagine you're driving along a back road in Florida and you see a bunch of oranges growing on trees in a large grove beside the road. What is the journey from those oranges on the tree to the delicious glass of orange juice sitting on the table in front of you for breakfast in the morning?

In other words, how do those oranges become everyday fruit for everyday use? It's a process, and until the owner of that grove takes the oranges through that process, you can't readily consume the juice in the morning.

What if every time you wanted a glass of orange juice with your breakfast, you had to get in your car, drive out to the orange grove, pick a crate of oranges by yourself, then bring them all back to your house and squeeze the juice out of them one at a time? It might be fun to do it once, but over and over again? Every morning? Think about all of the inefficiency and wasted time. If that was the only way to enjoy orange juice, you'd probably just give up on it.

But what if there was a process for harvesting all of those oranges, squeezing the juice out of them, bottling that juice, and delivering it to your house so you always had some on hand? Of course, that's exactly what orange juice companies do, and that's what Presentation Management does as well.

There's fruit hanging in folders all over your company, and your first step is to pluck all of that fruit and bring it together in one place. The next step is to process all of that fruit into an easily consumable form—like metaphorical bottles of juice—so everyone can consume it when they want. It's tedious work on the front end that saves your entire organization a whole lot more work in the future.

In terms of your slides, you're going to meticulously track down all of the content throughout your entire organization and bring it all together, organizing it using some kind of content management system that gives it thematic structure and makes it accessible for your people when they need it.

You probably already use a few content management systems to store and organize files, such as Dropbox, SharePoint, and the Windows file system. Now, you're going to do something similar with all of your presentation content. The only difference is that all of the files you bring together will be formatted specifically as slides that are ready to present.

All files formatted as slides, ready to present.

That way, all of your marketing and sales content is ready to be used, reused, and repurposed. So if you have a Power-Point presentation with twenty-two slides, every one of those individual slides will become a separate piece of content that can be stored, managed, updated, and reused—on demand—right from your slide library.

All of your *stored* content becomes *productive* content, so you no longer have to go "hunting and gathering" through folders looking for individual pieces that you can splice together into a new slide deck. No longer will a useful file go dormant in some forgotten place once you've used it.

Imagine if you asked a question on Google, and instead of giving you a bunch of links to webpages that *might* contain the answer, it provided you with a slide that directly answered your question using text and media. That's the power of Presentation Management, and it's practically a whole new medium of communication.

ORGANIZING YOUR TANGLED MESS OF SLIDES

- **Find.** Collect your best files. Think of your most recent and best presentations. Maybe it was the CEO's keynote at a conference, the HR company history, master sales decks, technology overviews, and product development plans. Even training presentations may have valuable company info.

- **Curate.** Weed through the bullshit. Get rid of duplicate slides, bad fonts, wrong colors, old logos, old background templates, footers, and so on. Do this step-by-step, one slide and one file at a time. Transform those files into scenes that tell a cohesive story about your business—formatted and ready to present.

- **Table of Contents.** Put all of your files into a Structured Story, with a chapter for each division, topic, and subject.

As we said, when you start going through all of your folders and gathering up content for your slide library, you're going to be amazed at the sheer amount of reusable and relevant files you already possess: videos you'd forgotten about, old slide presentations that were never used again, pictures you thought you'd lost, graphs and charts you've never seen before.

The VP of sales at Brighthouse described this process as "striking gold in our own backyard."

She discovered that they had a vast treasure trove of productive files at their fingertips. Think about how this is going to boost productivity. Think about how much more effectively and consistently people throughout your organization will be able to communicate in their presentations. Think about how powerful it's going to be when every single employee can respond to any customer question or concern within seconds using content that is already formatted and ready to present.

Once all of your content is organized into a slide library, you're ready to transform it into a story: the story of your company. When every presentation becomes a story, and every slide becomes a scene, we call that *Structured Storytelling*, and it's going to radically improve the way you communicate the value of what you have to offer.

With Structured Storytelling, the average sales rep can create stories with impact that leave customers feeling moved, fulfilled, inspired—or whatever you want them to feel.

CHAPTER 5

THE CULTURE OF PRESENTATION MANAGEMENT

MEDLINE IS ONE OF THE LARGEST MANUFACTURERS AND distributors of medical supplies in the world, with thousands of products. If you've ever used crutches, a wheelchair, medical gloves, gauze bandages, or any other type of hospital-quality medical supplies, there's a good chance you've used products by Medline.

According to Tanja Zaric, Senior Content Market Manager on Medline's marketing operations team, the company has nearly two thousand sales reps across numerous divisions and sales segments. When their sales reps make a presentation, they have a huge, highly detailed, and technical set of information that they have to convey, and each presentation must be tailored for the specific needs of each client.

For many years, they had product managers putting together beautiful, polished presentation slides, but there wasn't a central library where all of these slides could be readily accessed. As a result, there was a huge and ever-growing amount of content on the company's intranet, which meant reps often had to look in several places in order to find the most up-to-date and approved versions of slides.

This made it a bit inconvenient to create a consistent story across all of their sales divisions, and consistency is vitally important to an esteemed medical supply company like Medline. When they communicate information to the public, whether they're sharing financial numbers or product information, they are always careful to ensure that everything has been fully vetted by their regulatory team for compliance issues.

Additionally, the Medline brand has evolved over the years, so content has been regularly updated and refreshed. For all of these reasons, leaders knew they needed to somehow bring together all of their presentation content in a way that ensured structure, order, and consistency at all times, while also making up-to-date slides conveniently available to sales reps in every circumstance.

It was clear to leaders that accomplishing this was going to take more than a single project. It was going to require the right platform, the right training, and a whole new presentation culture—a culture in which presentations were treated with the same meticulous care, consistency, and oversight as any other major form of marketing communication.

When the company went through a rebranding, it seemed like the best time to get started. They decided to use our Shufflrr Presentation Management platform because it could quickly and efficiently roll out the change in branding to everyone in the field. As they trained team members on the new brand, they also taught them a new Presentation Management culture.

According to Tanja, they structured their slide library like the table of contents in a book, where each of their more than twenty sales divisions, representing products and capabilities that are marketed to different sales segments, had its own chapter. Each chapter was populated with relevant slides for the sales reps in those divisions. They further subdivided the chapters into sales segments, and then imposed a hierarchy that was logical to sales reps so they would never again have to spend a lot of time looking for relevant slides.

This was particularly important in the early days of the change, as reps learned to use the slide library and got acquainted with search functionality. Medline wanted reps to quickly embrace the new tool as they navigated this whole new culture of Presentation Management, so they made the transition as logical and easy to adopt as possible.

That little bit of extra work up front has been well worth it, because Medline now has better and more focused communication, a central resource of branded, consistent content for sales reps to easily create impactful and visually appealing presentations in minutes. While sales reps focus on selling, content strategists design, create, and update the slide decks, envisioning the company's overarching story and considering carefully how each slide fits into it.

The sales reps can easily find the specific presentation slides that they need, trusting that they have the most up-to-date information at all times. It doesn't feel like marketing is forcing content onto them. Rather, they are simply being helped so they can focus their efforts on what they do best.

A CRITICAL COMPONENT FOR EVERY CAMPAIGN

Presentation Management is more than a process, tactic, or approach—it's actually a culture that impacts your entire organization for the better, a strategy that treats presentations as a critical component of your sales, marketing, and advertising campaigns.

Every medium of communication has its own culture, if you think about it, with its own production processes, lingo, and experiences. And there are two sides to that culture: the strategic creative side, and the actual production process. Consider the culture of print media. First, you're identifying your audience, gathering information, writing copy, designing layout, meeting deadlines, and selling ad space— that's the strategic creative process. Then you have the actual printing and distribution of the newspaper, which involves a printing press, processes, and deadlines, as well as the tactile reality such as the sound of the machines, the smell of ink, and trucks arriving at the crack of dawn to pick up the newspapers. All of these elements together, from both the creative side and the production side, combine to create a print media culture.

And this isn't limited to communications. The same goes for architecture, which has both the strategic creative process that results in a blueprint, and the production process, in which construction crews and carpenters actually build the thing. The same goes for the culture of cooking, which involves the strategy of creating recipes and bringing together ingredients, and then the process for making the food. In all of these examples, the various processes and experiences for both the strategic creative side and the actual production come together to create a culture.

The same is true of presentations. There's a specific culture around Presentation Management that involves both a strategic creative side and the publishing and delivery of the presentation. This culture has its own processes, lingo, experiences, and approach. We're not creating this culture—we're merely identifying it. And it's a culture that is evolving naturally as companies develop and embrace new ways to manage their presentation communications.

> We're not creating this culture—we have identified it.

In many organizations, there's usually one person who is really good at creating presentations, and everyone goes to that individual for help and support when they need to create a slide deck. However, in a culture of Presentation Management, everyone gains the ability to present effectively because they are empowered through Structured Storytelling. They can do it themselves.

That one person in your organization who has been the go-to for presentations becomes a guru who helps everyone unleash the real potential of the slide library, but they no longer have to act as a crutch. Every team member becomes an expert at presentations, able to communicate the company's story clearly and respond to client questions and concerns at a moment's notice.

"Presentations stand out as one of the most effective forms of persuasion because they provide the best opportunities for intimacy and engagement. Now, you can manage them on an enterprise level."

—**Bob Jeffrey,** Worldwide Chairman and CEO,
J. Walter Thompson (retired)

The Language of Presentation Management Culture

The culture of Presentation Management, like any culture, has its own language and way of communicating. This language is what we call *Structured Storytelling*. With Structured Storytelling, every presentation tells a story, and every slide is a scene in that story. Additionally, there's always an emotional component combined with the logical component of any message. Emotion comes first, and then logic is used to reinforce the emotion.

Emotion + Logic

The structure typically looks like this: first you present a moving story, then you share the facts, then you close the deal. Some media companies do this very well. We first noticed this when we worked with NBC to present the Olympics to advertisers back in the late 1990s. NBC's presentation led with a video of Muhammad Ali at the Atlanta Summer Olympics in 1996, his whole body shaking from Parkinson's disease as he lit the Olympic torch. It was a powerful story that moved the audience. Reps then followed the story with the "numbers."

Lead with emotion, reinforce with logic. That's the language of Presentation Management. Why? *Because emotion creates motion.* Emotion is visceral. It grabs the audience like a hook and gets them to act, then logic and information give them justification for taking that action.

"Wow, the Olympics can be really moving and powerful," they say. "I would love for our brand to be associated with stories like this. And, oh, look at the viewership. It's also a good investment to advertise on the Olympics, according to these ratings."

That's the progression of thought when using Structured Storytelling. You are trying to create an emotional connection with your audience, and then following it up with facts and figures to give a logical purpose for those emotions. Of course, this is just one component of Structured Storytelling, but it's an important one.

At the same time, the language of Presentation Management *follows* the conversation, it doesn't *force* the conversation, because once you've created emotional momentum in your audience, you want to go with them on the journey.

Imagine you're on a Zoom call with a few clients. One of them brings up a topic related to one of your products, and, as it turns out, you already have some graphics in a folder on that topic. So, you open the folder, pull out the graphics, and share them on your screen with the clients right then and there. The graphics reinforce the conversation, and they help both you and your client make the point. It's a fluid, spontaneous conversation, not a forced, rigid slideshow—active participation instead of passive reception.

THE LANGUAGE OF PRESENTATION MANAGEMENT

- Every presentation is a story; every slide is a scene.

- Lead with emotion; reinforce with logic.

- Let the presentation follow the conversation, not force it.

If you're a CEO, then you are probably the best presenter in your company, the one person who can most clearly articulate your brand value. Embracing the culture of Presentation Management will empower *everyone* in your company to speak as intelligently and articulately as you about your products and services. At the same time, every piece of marketing content in your entire organization is now formatted as a slide, ready to present, so every team member, from the most outgoing and charismatic to the shyest introvert, has the tools and information they need to present clearly to any colleague, client, customer, partner, or investor at any moment.

Nobody has to build or rebuild slides every time they present, because once a slide has been created, it is readily available to be used over and over again. And because you can search through slides visually, you're never looking for the proverbial needle in a haystack. You can find the file you want much faster, which makes reusing slides and customizing presentations more efficient. This, in turn, ensures that every level of your organization from the CEO on down can articulate the same on-brand message with the same language and data.

This culture of Presentation Management has enabled every member of Medline's enormous team—all two thousand sales reps throughout the world—to sell a vast and highly technical range of products to a wide array of healthcare professionals with many different needs. And every single one of those reps is telling a consistent story about the brand, with the same lingo and the most current information.

Now, instead of slides being created by sales reps for a single presentation then disappearing forever into some folder on the network, every slide—every scene in every presentation—has an evolving life cycle that allows them to continue telling the company's story. And to become more effective and impactful over time.

Let's take a look at that life cycle next.

CHAPTER 6

THE LIFE CYCLE OF A PRESENTATION

According to Yvonne Stacherski, Senior Marketing Operations Manager, Vice President at Comerica Bank, the company's culture of sales presentations used to be "like the Wild West." Salespeople were creating their own sales decks from scratch, which means they were collecting their own content. There was broad inconsistency across presentations, and a lot of inappropriate, even goofy images being used.

Salespeople would use SmartArt, icons, their own photos—whatever they happened to have at their own disposal. "The Comerica brand and core values weren't always being represented properly, and this became a source of ongoing frustration for the marketing team."

While the company certainly wanted the brand to be represented accurately in the marketplace, there was an additional and more serious compliance risk to this Wild West approach. For a financial institution like Comerica, disclosures are crucial to compliance. There was a major concern that salespeople weren't being diligent in updating disclosures in their presentations, but company leaders didn't have a way to audit presentations as a whole. Further complicating the issue, if a disclosure changed for one line of business, it might cross multiple lines of business.

This created a real risk for the organization, not just a risk to their reputation but the potential of legal and regulatory sanctions. Ultimately, it became the primary driver in seeking a system that would give the company better control over their presentations.

Comerica adopted the Shufflrr Presentation Management system because they wanted something that gave them holistic control of their presentations but was flexible enough to meet the needs of every division in the company. For example, their wealth and commercial divisions needed to be able to change out company names and insert logos to make more personalized content for clients.

At the same time, they needed a system of record for their presentations so internal auditors could ensure at any point in time that everything was compliant. With Shufflrr, they had the ability to set appropriate permissions throughout the organization, and it also created a chain of custody for presentation communications.

Finally, they wanted technology that enabled their sales reps, and others, to interact with sales presentations anywhere.

As Yvonne put it, "We wanted high-quality, interactive sales presentations anytime, anywhere."

"We wanted high-quality, interactive sales presentations anytime, anywhere."

–Yvonne Stacherski, Senior Marketing Operations Manager, Vice President at Comerica Bank

As soon as Comerica embraced Structured Storytelling and began creating their own slide library, they discovered how much easier it is to create and manage presentations. They decided the best way they could help users was to structure their slides into chapters, with each chapter dedicated to one of the company's divisions: retail banking, business banking, and wealth management.

Recently, they did a brand refresh, and they discovered that their Structured Storytelling library makes it incredibly easy to transition to the new look and feel. Their brand redesign gave them a newer, more contemporary look, but it meant all of their slides had to be updated in a rather short period of time.

Under the old approach, this would have been impossible because all of the files throughout the network were not accounted for. Now they have the tools for each department to go in and update their content and republish it. They can each work in their own separate folders, and as long as the library is active, changes will be implemented at the same time across the organization.

Once the changes are implemented, the updated slides are placed in new folders, and the permissions on the old folders are simply turned off. That way, when a team member logs in and looks for slides, everything they see has the new look and feel. The company doesn't have to worry about someone accidentally pulling out an old slide with the old look. Think about it like pulling an old book off the shelf in a library and replacing it with a newer edition. From that point on, anyone who accesses the book will be pulling the new one off the shelf.

AN EVOLVING CYCLE

All of this provides an example of the endless circular life cycle that slides go through with Presentation Management.

The first step in the life cycle is ***creation***. As the name suggests, this refers to the act of creating slides and other content for presentations. Ideally, in a Presentation Management system, slides are created by content admins, usually someone in marketing. Content admins make sure that every piece of content is formatted as a slide, and that every slide is on brand and on message. They also set controls in the library for things like font and color.

The admins organize everything into chapters and folders that tell the corporate story. Much like the table of contents in a book, each chapter is clearly defined. You can go back and look at the table of contents at the beginning of this book to see an example of a structured story presentation of each chapter.

With Comerica, there is a chapter for each division of their company. A pharmaceutical company might have a chapter for each scientific area, then a subchapter for each disease state. A media company might have chapters for each network and subchapters for each show. A hotel chain might have chapters for each brand, from luxury to economy. A manufacturing company might have one chapter for materials, another for distribution, and other chapters for products. And so on. Typically, a company will also have a chapter-folder for their company history, a chapter-folder for marketing materials, a chapter-folder for sales, for R & D, and perhaps a chapter for investors.

When we worked with Mercedes-Benz, their structured story included chapters for *Safety, Innovation, Performance,* and *Style and Design*. Notice they led with concepts and ideals rather than car models and pricing. Products and prices change every day, but your company mission, ideals, and brand stay constant. They are at the core of the story—they are the presentation. The specifics about cars and pricing are slides—they are the scenes. Every presentation is a story, and every slide is a scene.

Once a slide is created, it is **distributed** through your Presentation Management system into the cloud to be accessed *and reused* by anyone with permission. This goes hand in hand with **sharing**, when content is made available to people inside and outside of the enterprise. When a user accesses the slide library at this point, it's a bit like shopping on Amazon. You find your relevant folder, pick the slides you want, put them in your slide cart, and hit save. Then you're out the door. The content admins make it that easy for you.

Let's suppose you're a salesperson getting ready for a presentation in Mexico. All you have to do is log into the slide library, and all of the content will already be organized and formatted for you. It's presented to you visually as well, so you're not hunting through file names for the right slide. You open relevant folders based on theme, select appropriate slides, and click and drag them into your slide cart. You can also use a search feature to find specific slides by keyword, and the search results are presented visually as well.

Let's suppose you're looking for a specific white paper about regulatory changes to your industry. You open the search bar and type, "Regulatory changes," and a few relevant slides appear in your search results. Because they're visual, you can quickly scan, find the specific white paper you want, then drag and drop it into your slide cart. It's as simple as that. The white paper is already formatted, on brand, and on message, so it's ready to go. However, you can edit the slide with some additional customizations tailored to your presentation, if you want—perhaps a bit of information relevant to a specific client.

Do the same for the rest of the slides in your presentation, then save it, and you're ready for *presenting*. Now you have a few options: present in person with a face-to-face meeting; broadcast your presentation remotely through Zoom, Teams, Skype, or WhatsApp; or send a secure, encrypted link and let the audience look at your slides on their own time. Presentation Management software will send you a notification when the file is opened, as well as which slides are looked at and for how long.

Social refers to the comments and feedback you receive after a presentation, which you can then respond to, as well as internal comments and feedback from your team about slides. In a face-to-face meeting, this might take the form of direct questions and comments on the content of specific slides. With a structured slide library, you have easy access to additional slides so you can respond to this feedback right then and there. Instead of "Let me get back to you about that," you get to say, "I have some information about that right here."

Then there's **reporting**, which means the internal and external gathering of data about how content is being used to better understand what's most effective. With good Presentation Management software, you can track, audit, and analyze your slides to see who presented what, when, and where. You'll know who the best presenters are, and you'll see what clients are responding to most strongly. In fact, you can track what is resonating most powerfully with clients in *real time*, down to the individual time spent on specific slides.

While *social* gives you anecdotal feedback—what people say—*reporting* gives you analytical feedback—what people actually do. Together, they provide emotion *and* logic, which are both critical for telling a story and turning emotion into motion.

"I see our best presenters spend an average of ten minutes on this particular slide, then seven minutes on this widget, but they tend to skip this other slide over here."

It's feedback and data more powerful than any focus group or research survey about client interests, and you can use it for **updating** and improving slides accordingly. Slides that are effective can be made *more* effective, while slides that don't work can be retired. You can create more of the content that's impactful, and clean out the stuff that never gets used (or shouldn't be used).

As you edit and update content, the updates are pushed out to every user's presentation. For example, if you change pricing information on a slide, it will be changed in every individual presentation that uses your slide library. This ensures that every presentation has current, relevant, and consistent information. There's a parent–child relationship between the slides in the slide library and the slides in individual presentations, which plays an important role in the slide life cycle. Additionally, when you present data from research companies (e.g., stock prices from Morningstar), the data gets updated by the minute, so it's always current in the child slide.

We will go into more detail about this parent–child relationship in Chapter 10, when we examine the genealogy of slides.

That brings us back around to **creation**, and the life cycle starts all over again. As Bob Davis, Associate Vice President of Marketing for HealthTrust Purchasing Group, put it, "Our presentations never finish."

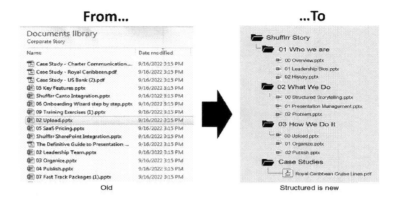

Under the old linear slide system, content exists on network folders, new folders tend to get created over time, and nothing gets deleted or cleaned out, so after a few years, you have a giant mess. Now there's a constant evolution so content gets improved or retired constantly through the publishing process.

We can all relate to working on SharePoint sites and network folders, watching them get bigger and messier over time as people add more and more content without regard to quality or usefulness. With a culture of Presentation Management, slides follow a distinct life cycle that keeps them relevant and easy to find, with correct information that is regularly updated to meet the most current needs of the organization.

Anything that's in the library has been approved by all the requisite departments (legal, marketing, product development, et al.), and the content design is current, so any rep can pull it out and use it without worrying if it's correct in every aspect. With Presentation Management, your slide library will never be messy again, and compliance issues are a thing of the past, because it's being managed, and every slide is a living, breathing piece of communication.

Every slide is a living, breathing piece of communication.

EVER-EVOLVING AND UPDATING FILES

So, what does this life cycle do for your presentations? It makes your slide library a living, breathing thing that evolves along with your company, so your team never again has to fumble around or waste time trying to put together brand-new presentations from scratch. Additionally, everyone is always using the right information about your company and telling a consistent, unified story.

Consider the example of Comerica. Through their brand refresh, they were able to keep every presentation consistent with updated information, logos, fonts, colors, and more, because every slide is updated globally when the parent slide is updated. That means they could roll out changes to the entire organization as they saw fit. They no longer had to worry about some individual in the organization accidentally continuing to use out-of-date content.

But Structured Storytelling takes it a step further. Imagine presentations that are connected to live data so they are constantly updated. For example, a slide showing the performance of the stock market could be connected to the stock exchange so it always has current stock prices, or a slide about the weather connected to the National Weather Service to show the latest forecasts in your area. The moment someone opens the slide, they see the most current data.

We spoke to Kurt Dupont of PresentationPoint about this aspect of Presentation Management. He has spent just as many years as we have working on presentations, but his primary focus is adding live data to slides and automating them. As an expert on the use of live data in slides, we've worked closely with him over the years. Here is what he had to say.

> Evidence is always convincing. Properly formatted data presentations are storytelling for evidence.
>
> We began to use live data twenty-five years ago, when we worked on creating real-time flight information for airport screens. For a long time, PowerPoint presentations were static, so we created a plug-in called DataPoint that enables users to connect their presentations to twenty-five different data providers. Now

presentations can connect shapes like text boxes, tables, graphics, and charts to databases that provide regularly updated information. As soon as a user opens a presentation, the latest information from relevant data sources is applied.

For example, a McDonald's franchise might create a presentation with their menu options that displays on restaurant screens, and a direct connection to headquarters will constantly update menu items and prices. This could be done at every McDonald's restaurant around the world, ensuring that every screen is being updated in real time, and the presentations can be customized for individual locations, so the display will be different at a McDonald's in Singapore versus a McDonald's in Kansas City.

This also allows for what is called 'mail merging,' where you can maintain a constantly updated list of slides for every product you sell in your database. In a presentation, you could show information like *number of items sold last week* or *current product pricing*, and it would all be updated as soon as you opened the slide. Additionally, you can create personalized presentations for each customer based on the products they are interested in, and the product information will be up-to-date with the latest images, pricing, and so on. In fact, this is how insurance companies generate customer proposals for individual clients.

The point is, slides can be database-driven; customized according to time, place, and location; and targeted to a specific audience. Imagine a hospital with twenty different locations. A patient enters one of those locations, and a display screen greets him with personalized information: "Welcome, Jacob. Your physician, Dr. Bob Schwartz, is ready to see you in room 125."

Your presentation can also be scheduled along a specific timeline, not unlike television programs on a broadcast cable network. So maybe the menu at the restaurant changes at a specific time of the day when the kitchen shifts from breakfast to lunch.

You're controlling the message, data, and statistics on every screen at all times. From virtual church services to business signage, distance learning, financial planning, road signage, and military planning, the direct connection to live data empowers presentations in so many amazing ways, we can't possibly mention them all. Now your audience is able to make intelligent, informed decisions, and you know that you have the latest and most accurate data every time you open a presentation.

START CLEANING YOUR ROOM

The good news is you already have everything you need to get started. All you have to do is collect your best presentation content, bring it all together in a shared folder, and then begin organizing it. How do you begin cleaning a dirty room? First, you drag everything out into the open so you can begin to identify and organize it.

As you begin to organize your content into separate chapters, you will discover many files that need to be updated. You'll see gaps in your structured library. For example, you may realize, "We need more case studies! Let's start contacting clients to see if they will participate. Also, our office in Texas isn't represented anywhere."

You'll discover which new slides need to be created, what information needs to be updated, and which out-of-date or irrelevant content needs to be deleted. Once your content is formatted, updated, and organized, you're ready to publish it so the rest of your organization can access it.

Of course, there will probably be different user groups throughout your organization who need access to different slides, and you can set those permissions as well. Certain sections of your library may only be accessible to salespeople, or HR, or your training team, and some sections will only be accessible to your executive team. At Comerica, the banking group doesn't need access to the slides for the wealth management group because they're completely different lines of business. So, they will be pulling slides from different folders within the same global library.

All of these permissions are easy to add, remove, and adjust throughout the life cycle of each slide by your content admins, so that any individual user who accesses the slide library knows that the content available to them is content they're allowed to use. Permissions can be set per slide, per folder, and per user group, and there are two different stages of permissions: consumers and publishers. Consumers can access the slides for presentations, while publishers can also create and publish slides.

You might also begin connecting some of your slides to real-time data sources, so you know you always have the latest information. This is where a product like DataPoint can come into play.

This organization is such an important part of Structured Storytelling that we'll look at the process of uploading, organizing, and publishing in greater detail in the next chapter.

CHAPTER 7

PICK AND PRESENT

LET'S SUPPOSE YOU GET INVITED TO A FORMAL DANCE ON A Friday night. It's Friday afternoon, so you don't have a lot of time to get ready. You know you have a nice blue dress, some formal shoes, makeup, a curling iron, and everything else you need, but your room is a mess. As you step into your room to start looking for what you need, you're overwhelmed at the state of the place.

"How did it get this bad?" you wonder. "I'll never find what I need in all of this mess."

The truth is, that mess didn't happen overnight. It's the result of many years of clutter and disorganization, with stuff getting crammed in the corners, in closets and drawers, under the bed and dresser. Some of it is trash that needs to be thrown away, but most of it is comprised of your personal possessions that are simply in disarray. You never intended for your room to get this bad; it just happened a little bit at a time over the years due to your busy life and a lack of proper organizational structure.

Unfortunately, all of that disorganization makes the process of getting ready a huge ordeal. You have no choice but to dig through the mess trying to find what you need. While you think you know where your nice shoes might be, you haven't seen that blue dress in years. Your curling iron is somewhere in the dresser, you think, but your makeup is scattered all over the place. Tracking down everything you need so you can get ready for the dance is going to take hours of frantic effort.

When you finally locate the dress, it's in bad shape. It needs to be dry-cleaned, and a button needs to be replaced. Since you don't have time for that, you select a different dress, one that doesn't look nearly as nice. You know you won't feel as confident, but you don't have a choice. Also, you never find the one specific color of lipstick you wanted to use, so either you will have to buy a new tube or settle for some other color. Your dress shoes are scuffed and have to be polished, and the curling iron seems to have vanished into a parallel universe—you can't find it anywhere.

All of this takes up the entire afternoon, so by the time you finally head to the dance, you're frustrated and in a bad mood, hardly the best attitude to enjoy the evening.

Now, what if your room was neatly organized? What if the trash was thrown away, your makeup was arranged in a makeup drawer with specific trays for each category, and your clothes were hung up and grouped according to styles? You'd know exactly where to find that dress, and it would already be cleaned, repaired, and ready to wear. Your shoes would also be cleaned, polished, and placed in a shoe rack. You would be able to *pick* out your clothes and be *presentable* within minutes instead of hours, and you'd be in a much better mood when you finally headed to the dance.

Clearly, such a change could radically transform your life, making you more willing to attend events on the fly, more confident about your appearance when you turn up at social activities, and more responsive to friends who invite you to things. When you get ready for a date or some other event, instead of facing a frustrating messy process of trying to find everything you need, you now have a *very simple process* of picking what you need and presenting yourself as you see fit.

Instead of facing a frustrating messy process of trying to find everything you need, you now have a very simple process with just two steps: picking and presenting.

MANY BRANDS, ONE STORY

That's how it is with Presentation Management, and that's exactly what Jessica Bland, a marketing manager at Choice Hotels, discovered. Choice Hotels is a single company comprised of twenty different brands, including Clarion, Comfort, Sleep Inn, Quality Inn, Econo Lodge, and Rodeway Inn. Can you imagine the tangled mess of slides such a company could easily develop over time, with individual sales reps across twenty different brands constructing their own presentations and shoving content into folders all over the place?

And imagine the nightmare of trying to keep all of those presentations consistent across twenty brands with thousands of employees so that the company tells one overarching story about their brand! It would be a monumental task beyond the capacity of even the most talented team.

The marketing manager was tasked with creating a presentation for investors that was supposed to provide a compelling overview of the entire company and *each* of its twenty brands. Once upon a time, such an assignment would have been an invitation to hundreds of miserable hours of tracking down content, refreshing it, updating all of the brand information, and then bringing it all together.

"Well, I'll be staying late at the office tonight," the marketing manager might have thought. "And I'll be staying late tomorrow, too. Will I even be able to find all of the files I need? How much updating of slides am I going to have to do? How many new slides will I have to create from scratch, and how in the world am I going to get all of these slides to be perfectly aligned for a single presentation?"

That's how it might have been at Choice Hotels at one time, but not any longer! The company now uses a Structured Storytelling library, so when a marketing manager gets an assignment, they don't even bat an eye. They know it's only going to take about five minutes to create and output a presentation, with slides that are guaranteed to be relevant, on brand, and on message. And that presentation will provide a compelling overview of all twenty brands while telling a singular story about the company as a whole. Not only is it much easier to tell that singular story, but reps can also cross-sell other brands with ease. Here's how the process works:

The marketing manager goes right to their laptop, opens up the slide library, and all of the categories of content are readily accessible right there: master slides, individual brands, promotions, images, logos, videos, and more. They can go under each brand to draw slides for each one, knowing that every slide will already be aligned with the global company.

Within just a few minutes, they have found relevant, well-designed, and well-formatted slides for each of the twenty brands and dragged them into their presentation.

Then they add a slide at the end about the Choice Hotels corporation. They can also find content that shows what hotel rooms look like, what the restaurants look like, and slides that highlight the differences between each brand. The look and feel of every file they use is consistent, so slides already flow perfectly from one to the next. Plus, all photos, videos, logos, and information are current.

All the marketing manager has to do is click and drag each slide, put it into the equivalent of a shopping cart, then reorganize it into their presentation. From there, they can export it, and it's ready to go. They can now put it into their own presentation folder to be used when and where they want to use it.

"Well, that was easy," the marketing manager thinks. "Fifteen minutes and I'm ready for my presentation. No more late nights at the office!"

TWO SIMPLE STEPS

So, how would you react if you found out *right now* that you had a big presentation tomorrow morning? Would you panic? Get frustrated? Frantically start trying to find relevant content for your slide presentation?

"Well, I'll be working through the weekend," you might think. "This is going to be a nightmare."

With a Structured Storytelling library, getting ready for a presentation is a simple two-step process: *pick and present.*

That's it.

First, you access the slide library, where everything is neatly organized in chapters, so you can find what you need quickly and easily. *Pick* your slides and add them to your presentation. As we said, it's no more complicated than clicking and dragging an item into your shopping cart on an e-commerce website like Amazon. Then you save the presentation in your own presentation folder.

Now you can *present* your presentation at a moment's notice. And as we said in a previous chapter, you can use your slide deck to present in person, online, or by providing a secure link to your audience.

See how easy that was? Suddenly, it's not such a big deal for a global corporation like Choice Hotels to create high-quality presentations, even though it's a company comprised of twenty brands and thousands of individual hotels all over the world. All of the best content for all of those brands can be curated and brought together into one place, where anyone with permission can pick and present their own slide presentations as well.

Even if you suddenly discover that you have to present to your biggest client in one hour, you have no need to panic.

Everything you require for the presentation will be easy to find, organize, and present without any need to hunt around, panic, or create new slides. Just pick and present!

And if you have to respond to a client on the fly during a presentation, you can access additional content without any prep time at all. For example, let's suppose a salesperson representing Choice Hotels in a B2B environment meets with a group of travel agents to show them a slide deck depicting all of the different brands they offer. Suddenly, in the middle of the presentation, one of the travel agents asks an unexpected question.

"Sorry to interrupt, but do you have any hotels in Little Rock, Arkansas? That's where I'm located, and I'd really like to know what you have to offer in my area."

Again, there's no need to panic. The Choice Hotels salesperson simply opens their slide library, instantly accesses slides for the company's Little Rock hotels, and pulls them up.

"Yes, here are our hotels in Little Rock. As you can see, we have multiple Comfort Inn and Quality Inn locations. Plus, we have some Econo Lodge locations, if you have a tighter budget but still want a comfortable stay."

"How many of your Comfort Inn locations have conference rooms?" the travel agent asks.

"Let me show you that right now. Here are those locations, along with pictures of their conference rooms. And we've got pricing information for renting those conference rooms, as well."

"And can you show me a list of the amenities for each of those hotels?"

"Yes, of course; that information is right here on this other slide."

Again, it's no more complicated than pulling up pictures of your latest vacation on your phone. Just open the appropriate folder, scroll through the available content, and pull up what you need right then and there. The process of using a Structured Storytelling slide library couldn't be easier or more flexible. Freed from the inconvenience of the old linear slide system, you can now concentrate on making better presentations for everyone.

Indeed, with a bit of practice, you could easily become the Martin Scorsese of presentations. We'll show you how in the next chapter.

CHAPTER 8

MAKING BETTER PRESENTATIONS FOR EVERYONE

"THE OLYMPICS IS ABOUT MORE THAN GOLD MEDALS," Kerri Strug said. "It's about human spirit, the heart, and the drive that a lot of athletes have and human beings have in general."[5]

She should know. Her own story lives on in the memories of all who witnessed it (either in person or on television) in Atlanta in 1996. She was the last to vault for the United States gymnastics team. On her first attempt, she under-rotated, landed badly, and injured her ankle. Despite the injury, she received a score of 9.162, but she needed to land a second vault in order to clinch the gold.

---

5   Lily Kuo,"Gymnast Strug Motivates Others with Story of Gold," *Reuters*, 2012, https://www.reuters.com/article/us-oly-gymn-wstrug-idUSBRE85R0AQ20120628.

Honestly, nobody would have blamed her if she'd stopped there. She had a pronounced limp and was clearly in pain. However, Kerri decided to make a second attempt at the vault. It is a moment that has been played and replayed over and over again.

Kerri limps to the end of the runway and goes for her second vault, running full steam ahead. Somersaulting off the ramp, she lands perfectly on both feet, salutes the judges briefly, then collapses to her knees in agony.

The commentator, John Tesh, can be heard on the video saying, "Kerri Strug is hurt! She is hurt badly!"

For her second vault, she was awarded a 9.712 by the judges, which guaranteed the American team a gold medal.

Video of that final vault has been played countless times in the years since, and it always has an impact on the audience. Kerri's Olympic story, full of both determination and pathos, is far from unique. If you watch the Olympics, you've seen many of these kinds of stories, stories of athletes overcoming hardship, facing triumph and defeat, victory and disappointment, joy and pain. These kinds of stories give Olympic events even more gravitas, and the networks that air the Olympics know it.

It's the reason why the network gives you touching stories about athletes and the adversities they've overcome before you watch them compete. As we recounted earlier, legendary boxer Muhammad Ali appeared at the same 1996 Summer Olympics as Kerri Strug. Ravaged by Parkinson's disease, he mounted the steps and raised his trembling hand to light the Olympic torch.

A young salesperson at NBC first had the idea of using Muhammad Ali's emotional moment, and other moments like it, to sell the Olympics to advertisers. We were in the room when they made their presentation, and we watched the power of those videos firsthand. That salesperson had learned an important lesson: powerful stories tie your entire presentation together in a way that keeps your audience invested from beginning to end.

Now, we should point out, the emotional response to Kerri Strug's final vault varies, and it has changed somewhat over the years. At the time, it was mostly seen as a powerful example of willpower and sheer determination, but more recently, some find the video a troubling example of a young athlete being pushed too far by an overbearing coach. That's why it's important to understand both the emotional impact you *want* to make, as well as the impact you're *likely* to make on your target audience.

Choose and design your content wisely to achieve your desired effect. Know your audience, and be ready to pivot or adjust based on their reactions and feedback. That's what good storytellers always do. The presentation follows the conversation and reacts to the audience—Structured Storytelling makes this easy.

Powerful stories tie your entire presentation together in a way that keeps your audience invested from beginning to end.

THE MARTIN SCORSESE OF PRESENTATIONS

Structured Storytelling is about creating presentations that don't just throw information at people; they tell a compelling story. Your organized library makes it easier to tell more effective stories that move your audience, where every slide is a scene in that story, and every scene makes an emotional impact.

A celebrated director like Martin Scorsese doesn't include a scene in a movie like *Goodfellas*, *The Departed*, or *The Wolf of Wall Street* unless he knows what kind of emotion he wants to evoke in his audience. He considers very carefully how people are supposed to feel about each character, about each plot development, and he meticulously plans the layout of each scene. The scenes are strung together in such a way that they create an emotional resonance, which builds toward some overall feeling he wants to leave the audience with at the very end.

First, there's a happy scene where the main characters are having a good time. They tell jokes, laugh, and enjoy life. Then suddenly, there's a bloody and violent scene where one of those characters is brutally murdered. The juxtaposition of a happy mood with a violent act jars the audience. It grabs their attention and stirs their emotions. After that, we get a scene that shows the surviving characters racked with sadness and anger. Finally, we build toward a scene where the victim's friends seek revenge.

Each of these scenes creates emotion, builds suspense, and makes the story exciting for viewers, but strung together, they build an overarching emotional journey for the audience. By the climactic scene, the audience is rooting for the hero to get revenge in a bloodthirsty fashion and either celebrating his success or lamenting his failure.

We're not suggesting that your presentations need to create the same mood as a Scorsese film (although that might be interesting), but we *are* encouraging you to view presentations as yet another way to tell impactful stories to an audience.

Muhammad Ali lighting the Olympic torch wasn't just about kicking off the 1996 Olympic Games. It was a story of a once-great superstar athlete dealing with a debilitating disease who rose above the challenge to participate in a historic event. The will of the champion was still there in that frail body. NBC's Olympic salespeople included it in their sales presentations to advertisers because it was a powerful human story of triumph and tragedy, courage, and willpower, and it honored a great American hero. But it also provided an emotional context for understanding the power of running ads on Olympic broadcasts.

Evaluate each slide you use as a scene in a movie that is taking your audience on an emotional journey. What is your audience supposed to feel during the scene? How are they supposed to react emotionally to the content? Even if it's just a pie chart, consider what emotion it's supposed to evoke. How is that scene supposed to lead out of the slide before it and into the slide after?

When you make every slide a scene in a movie, then your product, service, or message becomes the hero of the story. Muhammad Ali wasn't the real hero of that video; the Olympics were. And the story of that hero goes something like this: "The Olympics creates powerful, moving, humanizing moments about drive, determination, and glory, overcoming adversity to succeed, as well as the agony of defeat. They show humanity at its most visceral. That's why people tune in. We don't watch just to see people run faster, jump farther, or throw a javelin. We watch because of those human stories of triumph and defeat. The power of those powerful human stories reflects very well on any brand, individual, organization, or nation associated with them."

When you make every slide a scene in a movie, then your product, service, or message becomes the hero of the story.

Most people feel anxiety about giving presentations because, in most linear presentations, the presenter is the focus. The presenter is the "hero" of the presentation. But when the *product, service,* or *message* becomes the hero of an emotional story, the focus is shifted off the presenter. Because they're telling a story and taking the audience through a series of scenes, not just trying to present dry information, they can relax a bit and let the story itself do some of the heavy lifting. The pressure is taken off the presenter and put back onto the product, service, or message, and once the pressure is off, it's a lot easier to present and talk with confidence.

The Muhammad Ali video, the Kerri Strug video, and other powerful moments from Olympic history created strong emotions in those sales presentations. Can you imagine how much harder it would have been for the presenter to create an equally strong reaction just from sharing ad numbers, market studies, and information about pricing?

Storytelling is one of the most effective tools in your toolbox for making better presentations that move, entertain, and inspire your audience. And your audience will be grateful for it. Nobody wants to sit and listen to a full presentation of data or a bland sales pitch, but every human being on earth resonates with stories.

Move, entertain, and inspire your audience.

If you want to stand in front of a room full of people and convince them to do something, a compelling story is always going to be the most effective way to do it. This is why lawyers tell stories in their opening and closing arguments during a trial. It's why American presidents include personal stories about real people in their State of the Union addresses. It's why companies use case studies.

Shift the focus from yourself to the real hero of the story: your product, service, or message. Take the audience through a story about that hero scene by scene, and build a narrative. Start with emotion, because emotion resonates with the audience, then follow with information. When you do this, the information gets tied to the emotion. Suddenly, all of those dry stats about viewing audience, cost, ROI, and so on get connected to moving moments like Muhammad Ali lighting the Olympic torch.

TRANSFORMING A SLIDE INTO A SCENE

So, how do you begin turning your slides into scenes that provoke some specific emotion in your audience? It may not sound easy to turn pricing information into an emotional scene, so here's a tip from one of our presentation designers:

"Begin with a thought-provoking statement, a headline, and connect it to a dramatic image or video. Remember, a picture paints a thousand words, but pictures also create a lot more emotion. Watching a video or looking at a picture is always more engaging than forcing someone to read text in a presentation format."

For each slide, ask yourself the following questions:

- Who is the hero of this slide and what is the hero trying to convey to the audience?

- How should the audience feel by the end of the slide?

- What knowledge should they have gained?

- How will they have moved along the story line of my presentation?

You can boil this down to five things that we can use to evaluate each slide: the *hero*, the *message*, the *feeling*, the *information*, and the *next action*. Once you've identified each of these things for a slide, find a visual to communicate them. Text alone is almost never powerful enough, so we recommend always looking for some visual to make your scene more effective.

In fact, it might be helpful to construct each individual slide as a *meme*, combining an image or video with provocative text designed to provoke a feeling, draw a contrast, or visualize a conflict. Think, for example, of the famous meme where a couple is holding hands, walking down a sidewalk, while the boyfriend turns and looked over his shoulder at another woman. That single meme communicates an entire story unto itself and creates an immediate emotional response in viewers.

That meme is called the "distracted boyfriend," and all kinds of quotes and phrases have been attached to the image to make a variety of points or social statements. For example, there's the one where the boyfriend is identified as "millennials," his girlfriend as "financial stability," and the other woman as "avocado toast." Depending on what generation you come from, you will have a variety of strong responses to that version of the meme.

Generally, memes are meant to encourage debate or provoke a response, but they can be used in many different ways as long as you're creative. You've probably seen the meme where the blonde woman is yelling and pointing at a distressed (or possibly confused) white cat, as the cat sits behind a dinner plate of what appears to be steamed vegetables. It's actually a juxtaposition of two unrelated images, the cat from Tumblr (his name is "Smudge") and the woman from an episode of *The Real Housewives of Beverly Hills* (her name is Taylor Armstrong). That single meme has been used thousands of times because, as silly as it is, it instantly creates a sense of conflict in a humorous way.

FIVE QUESTIONS FOR EVERY SLIDE

- Who is the hero of this slide/scene?

- What is the hero trying to convey to the audience?

- How should the audience feel by the end of the slide?

- What knowledge should they have gained?

- How will they have moved along the story line of your presentation?

WHAT STORY ARE YOU TELLING?

Memes are helpful for creating structure in a slide, but remember, a slide isn't just provoking a feeling, it's helping to tell a story. If you treat your presentation as a story, and each slide as a scene in that story, you are guaranteed to make a greater impact on your audience.

Instead of a disjointed series of slides, you will create motion as you move from slide to slide, taking your audience along on an emotional journey. Think of it this way: emotion creates motion. That's what storytelling does. It's really no different than what a great writer does. Each scene has a specific role to play in moving characters along the plotline toward a climax and resolution. Just apply that same thinking to your presentations, and it will all start to come together in a powerful way.

How does emotion create motion, practically speaking? First, you create an emotional scene, then you follow it up with data, and you conclude by telling the audience to do something. That's the motion you're creating: make your audience feel something through an emotional scene, reinforce that emotion by providing them with information or data, then ask them to do something as a result.

Let's suppose you're making a presentation for an engineering company that designs and manufactures brakes for automobiles. You start your presentation with an emotional scene that shows how brakes keep people from crashing. Maybe you tell a harrowing true-life story about a family that lost control on an icy road and almost slid into a ravine, but your company's brakes worked despite the ice and saved them at the last possible second. Then you provide some statistics on vehicle safety with your brakes. Then you encourage the audience to purchase your brakes. That's emotion creating motion.

Emotion creates motion.

The Muhammad Ali video that the NBC salespeople used was a powerful story all by itself. When that scene was placed within the context of the rest of the NBC sales presentation, it communicated the power of Olympic moments, the impact they make on a global audience, and the way they speak to the strength and nobility of great athletes. And that, of course, flows right into the overarching message: that advertisers would be tapping into a powerful message of human achievement by teaming up with the Olympics.

Based on the principles we've just described, an account executive with only two years of sales experience can take a powerful presentation like that and instantly become a great presenter, because the story alone does most of the hard work. Of course, there are many different ways that the Muhammad Ali video can be used within the presentation. It might work at the beginning as a way to set the emotional stage, or it might work better near the end, to drive home the impact of the message.

And even if the slide isn't included in the presentation initially, the presenter can decide on the fly to pull it out of the slide library.

"Oops, my audience seems to be losing interest in my presentation. I'd better pull that Muhammad Ali video out of the library so I can regain their full attention."

That's what we mean when we say your presentations become a conversation instead of just a linear slideshow. You're able to react to your audience to keep them invested in the story. If you need a sudden emotional component to bring them back, you can reach into your library, grab that video like your secret weapon, and play it.

Let's suppose your presentation is trying to convince an audience to invest in a school. There's a lot of dry information that needs to be shared, many different numbers to throw at the audience. Halfway through the presentation, you realize you're getting glazed-over looks from people, so you pull out a video of the championship football game from a few years back. It's a clip from when a local hero, the team's running back, won the game, a victory that led to him getting the Heisman Trophy. The video clip ends with his teammates carrying him off the field on their shoulders, while his parents cry tears of joy in the stands.

By sharing that video, you tell the heartwarming tale of a heroic moment and tie it to the larger story of the school's impact on students and the community. Suddenly, your audience feels invested in those numbers and the glazed-over looks go away.

"This story is what our school is all about. These triumphant moments in the lives of students and their families—that is what you're supporting when you invest in us."

James attended the University of Houston, and a high-light of his years at the school was watching Andre Ware win the Heisman Trophy in 1989. The night before the fateful game at Rice Stadium, James stayed up all night with friends printing T-shirts that said, "Where is the Heisman?" When it was announced that Andre had won, the cheerleaders all donned the shirts and flipped across the field.

Actually, the event is also notable for creating a bit of legal trouble. The first shirt design included Andre Ware's name, and a team of lawyers sent James a warning that this might make the player ineligible for award consideration. James and his friends scrambled to make a second design, which relied upon the homonym between "where" and "Ware" rather than using the player's name directly. And the rest is history.[6]

To this day, James can reference the Heisman experience when speaking to UH alumni across the nation to create an instantaneous emotional connection that evokes all kinds of happy memories. And, as we said, emotion creates motion.

Make every slide a scene, use compelling visuals, and tell a story that will resonate with your audience. That's how you create better presentations for everyone. With that understanding, you're ready to begin implementing Structured Storytelling throughout your organization.

---

6 "New York Event Inspires Confidence and Cougar Pride | Highlight Houston." University of Houston. http://development.uh.edu/highlight-houston/new-york-event-inspires-confidence-and-cougar-pride/.

PART 3

IMPLEMENTING STRUCTURED STORYTELLING

CHAPTER 9

THE EVOLUTION OF PRESENTATION

PRESENTATIONS DON'T END. THEY JUST EVOLVE.

Yesterday's presentation is merely an iteration for tomorrow's presentation, much like software is released in versions 1.0, 2.0, and 3.0, and each iteration ideally makes the software better. When you implement a structured slide library, your slides become iterative, getting better and more impactful over time, and once you've started asking the five questions from our last chapter about every slide in your library, every slide is transformed into a powerful piece of a narrative that helps to tell the story of your company to whomever your target audience happens to be.

Why does every slide get better and better? Because you reevaluate it every time you use it. Each slide gets tweaked over time in order to make it more effective. At the same time, your content admins use analytics to see which ones are working, which aren't working, and which are getting used the most.

Of course, slides play different roles. Some need to show the data: 2+2=4. Others need to be tearjerkers that bring your audience back to the human experience. Some need to provide pretty pictures that serve as transitions into or out of the data. However, over time, with analytics, tweaks, and adjustments, they will each get better at their individual roles.

SHOPPING FOR BETTER SLIDES

According to Yvonne Stacherski, Comerica's structured slide library has created a process of continual improvement that allows them to reuse marketing content repeatedly. Slides created for specific events or messages, including marketing data, images, graphics, and reports, are placed in the slide library for further use, which turns the library into a repository for the best curated content in the organization.

Now, when someone sits down to create a presentation, they can delve into the slide library, where all of the best content is already formatted, compliant, and ready to present, and they can, as Yvonne put it, "Go shopping for slides."

Each division within the same company uses the structured slide library, and while each of those divisions is managed independently with their own users in mind, the library enables the company to create a unified enterprise that is consistent, on brand, and on message. Cross-selling and upselling to clients are both easier than ever because the best content from each division is readily available at all times.

Every relationship manager has access to the slide library for their sales presentations, so any of them can conduct a quick search to pull relevant sales materials from another division into their presentation and speak intelligently about it. At the same time, they can conduct granular analysis of presentation usage, which allows for better strategizing.

However, perhaps the most compelling aspect of Comerica's transition to a Structured Storytelling library is how it helped them navigate their rebranding effort. They didn't want to present multiple brands in the marketplace, because that could confuse clients and customers. They had to rebrand quickly across all of their materials out in the marketplace, an especially daunting task with so many divisions.

Updating the brand, logos, and look of the slides in their library caused an evolution in presentations that impacted the entire organization. The updates flowed out to every user in every division as a kind of natural evolution. At the same time, Comerica had to update all of their print ads and public signage, which took a lot longer and proved quite a bit more challenging.

Initially, they expected the rollout to take close to a year, but ultimately, it only took a couple of months to move their business units through the new branding experience. The overall graphic design of every slide was immediately changed and distributed in a very efficient manner—something that would have been unthinkable with the messy old approach to presentations.

Indeed, it took longer for their internal technology partners to push the new template out in PowerPoint than it did for Shufflrr to transition hundreds of slide decks. This is just one example of how improvements made in a structured slide library become improvements for the entire organization, and since slides are constantly getting tweaked, refined, and adjusted, presentations are constantly being improved for everyone in the enterprise.

"The brand was updated with precise accuracy and precise timing."

–Yvonne Stacherski, Comerica Bank

Let's suppose you gave a presentation last summer that included an anecdote. A few months later, you realize there's an even better anecdote you could have used to make the same point more effectively, so you change the specific slide. From now on, anyone who pulls that slide for a presentation will have the better anecdote, and anyone who has used it in the past will now have the newest version.

But what if a change is made that isn't an improvement? Suppose, for example, that you discover your CEO's name has been misspelled on a key slide. Because of the analytics in your slide library, you can look and see exactly when that change was made and by whom. In fact, you can see an image of each slide before and after a change was made. In this case, you can see exactly how the spelling of the CEO's name got changed. This makes it easier to update slides for distribution, weeding out bad or old versions and replacing them with newer and better slides.

This pinpoints the exact moment and cause of any problems and makes it easier to both fix the problem and prevent them in the future. The permission structure of your slide library allows you to decide who has access to make changes to particular slides, which creates a chain of custody. That way changes aren't being made haphazardly without any oversight, and because you know the chain of custody, you know how to avoid it going forward.

In the past, if a slide got changed in a bad way, you usually didn't know how it happened, how long it had been that way, who did it, or why. That made it very hard to introduce better processes that would prevent mistakes and improve communication.

MANAGED EVOLUTION

The big-picture value of this kind of slide evolution is clear: your presentations become marketing assets that change, improve, and evolve along with your business. Much like your website, where you can track views, requests, and progress; make changes accordingly; and do it all again next month. When you release a new product, it gets added to your website, and your website evolves. The same goes for your presentations.

Every slide and every presentation becomes a continually evolving marketing asset. They are no longer "one and done." You don't create a presentation from scratch for next week's meeting, then throw it away once the meeting is over and create a whole new presentation for the next meeting. And because it's a core communication tool, it affects your bottom line.

> Your presentations become marketing assets that change, improve, remain relevant, and evolve along with your business.

Just like your website, PR strategy, and advertising strategy, your *Presentation Management strategy* should be planned at the highest level of your company, not left to account executives to constantly wing it. After all, presentations are given when someone is being asked to make a decision about buying your product. Why would you leave it to account executives to constantly start from scratch and try to figure it out? The messaging, imagery, and graphics in your structured slide library need to be planned at the highest level, and they should be constantly evolving.

> Presentations are given when someone is being asked to make a decision about buying your product.

Presentations are now a vital element in your marketing mix, not an afterthought. Put another way, Presentation Management ends up becoming a line item on a corporate balance sheet, just like CRM, advertising, billboards, your website, and other forms of marketing. And if it's a line item, then there should be a real budget allocated to it every year from now on.

Since presentations are used during key moments of decision-making, they are worth the investment of time and resources to ensure that your global organization is in sync, everyone telling the right story in the right way with the right information at all times. They're communicating consistently and they're communicating better and better over time.

Unlike natural evolution, which is the result of unguided natural selection, the evolution of slides should be managed so that they change along with the company, stay on message, and become more effective over time. You have the knowledge and analytics to see what is working and what needs improvement, so you can tweak and improve slides to keep them current and make them better.

You can also communicate to your people about which slides are working best.

James has owned an iPhone since 2010, so when he opens the Photos app, he has immediate access to pictures of his son from age four to age fifteen—the entire time frame that he's owned an iPhone. The history of his son is all right there, already placed in folders according to name, date, location, and more.

In seconds, he can pull up a picture of his son at a Rangers game in 2010. Then he can pull up a picture of his son from his sophomore year in high school. It's all available and accessible within seconds, and because he still takes pictures of family activities, the photos stay current.

The same is true of your slides in a Structured Storytelling library. They're staying up to date, evolving to get better and follow changes in your company, but you can also track changes and see the whole history of your presentations. You know what's changed, when it changed, and who changed it.

That's the power of Presentation Management, transforming your slides into real marketing assets that grow and improve over time, an ever-evolving tool that you can use strategically just like any other marketing asset.

CHAPTER 10

THE GENEALOGY
OF A SLIDE

"Wow, that baby looks just like his mommy! Same hair color, same smile."

"That young man is a great baseball player, just like his father. His dad led his team to the Little League World Series in 1985, and it looks like Junior might do the same this year."

"Has anyone ever told you that you have the same weird sense of humor as your dad?"

"You have such a strong soprano singing voice. Your mother does, too. In fact, there are a lot of talented singers in your family."

It makes sense that we should inherit traits from our parents. After all, we are literally created from DNA passed down to us from our father and mother. From a genetic standpoint, the parent–child relationship is unavoidable. Sometimes it's a good thing, as when a child inherits a certain talent or skill. Other times, it can be bad, as when a child inherits a genetic defect or disease.

There's a similar parent–child relationship with Presentation Management, except it's more direct and, as long as content admins do their job well, it's only ever a good thing. Here's how it works.

When you create a presentation using a structured slide library, every new presentation is, by definition, comprised of duplicate slides, called "child slides," from the published slide library. The original slide in the library is the "parent slide," and the relationship between parent and child is an important aspect of Presentation Management.

While every child slide will reflect changes made to its parent slide, each child can be tracked individually. The full history of every child slide is available, so if a slide is used three hundred times, you can track exactly where it was used. You can see that it was used thirty-eight times in HR presentations, forty-five times in sales presentations, and so on. At the same time, because changes to parent slides are always reflected in child slides, every update made by content admins is reflected in every presentation throughout your organization.

Let's suppose you have a slide that provides an overview of your company, and in that slide, you refer to yourself as "an international company." For rebranding purposes, company leaders decide to change that phrase to "a global company."

"We have to roll out this change of phrase to the entire organization," they say.

To do this, a change is made to the parent slide. Up until now, that overview slide has been used 225 times in presentations throughout your organization in all kinds of contexts and for all kinds of reasons. That means there are 225 child slides contained within various presentations. However, as soon as you make the change to your parent slide, as soon as "an international company" becomes "a global company," the text is updated in every child slide, and every user gets a notification about the update.

At the same time, every parent slide maintains an ancestry of data that can be accessed with analytics and reporting, and that information becomes critical business intelligence about what's working and what isn't. You know which slides are being used, when, where, and by whom, which slides are being updated and which are not, which slides get reused frequently and which do not. All of this information creates a knowledge base like nothing you've had before. As you track the genealogy of your slides, you gain a clear understanding of how your global organization is communicating, and you can adjust accordingly.

ONE BIG, HAPPY FAMILY

Imagine being able to click on a slide inside of a presentation and instantly see who its parent slide is or, if it *is* the parent, how many children it has produced. Imagine being able to see exactly who made each of those child slides and where they currently reside and how many times they've made an appearance.

In a sense, the parent slide provides the DNA that transfers to each of the child slides. Of course, this relationship can be spun out to additional generations. For example, there might be a grandparent slide, which is used to create parent slides for specific groups in your company, who then create child slides from them for their presentations. No matter how many generations there are, however, they can all be tracked precisely. It's a big, happy family of slides where everyone gets along.

And remember, when we say *slide*, we're talking about *all* of your PowerPoint files, every single piece of content in your library—pictures, video, charts, graphs, white pages, PDFs, everything—because every piece of content is automatically formatted as a slide, ready to present. Indeed, we could use the terms "file" and "slide" interchangeably here.

Put another way, it's a content management system for your presentations in which every file is part of a big, happy family with a parent–child relationship. If you create a meme and place it in your library, you will be able to track every time it is reused (i.e., all of its children): who used it, where it was used, how it was set up, and the context in which it was used. You'll be able to track how people responded to each child. Did they buy the product? Did the presenter follow up with another emotional slide that led to a sale?

Through this intergenerational slide analysis, you can understand the effect and impact of every slide on a global scale, and you're able to continually edit parent slides to make them more efficient. Indeed, the very purpose of creating child slides every time someone uses the parent slide in a presentation is precisely so you have analytics about which slides are being used and how effective they are.

You can click on any slide in your library and see its entire ancestry: who its parents were, where it came from, if it was duplicated, how many times it has been shown, who showed it, whether or not it was in front of a client. Was it altered? Which presentations was it a part of? Which salespeople are using it? How long did a client look at it? If a salesperson sends the same presentation to ten different clients, you can see how much time each client spent on each slide in that presentation.

It's an incredible amount of data that provides tremendous accountability for the activity of each slide. You get insight into the chain of custody for each slide and 100 percent data integrity about who did what, when, and where, which enables you to figure out which slides are best and which components of each slide are most valuable. And if each slide is a scene, as we said before, you can determine where each scene belongs in order to create better storytelling.

If a salesperson is going off in their own direction, you'll know it. In fact, you will be able to help everyone get on the same page, pointing to the same horizon and sailing to the same destination with their presentations.

> You open a door to understand how presentations impact communication throughout your global organization.

All of this data allows you to continually tweak and improve your slides, as you learn over time what works and what doesn't. Of course, that process requires careful reporting and analysis, which we'll talk about next.

CHAPTER 11

REPORTING AND ANALYSIS

A HEAVY BURDEN LAY ON THE SHOULDERS OF SPECTRUM Networks salespeople in the days before Presentation Management.

Spectrum is the local programming division of Charter Communications, representing more than ninety-one dedicated, hyperlocal news and sports networks. Salespeople had to regularly conduct presentations for local advertisers in markets across the country[7]. To make this particularly difficult, every single market had its own ratings, and those ratings changed every night depending on what people watched on each area's local stations.

For example, a Spectrum salesperson might go to a car dealer in Rochester and say, "Look at how good the ratings

---

7 "About Spectrum Networks | Charter." Corporate.charter. https://corporate. charter.com/spectrum-networks.

were for our local channels last night. If you'd bought time on our channels, you would have gotten a great deal." And that was essentially how they marketed for their entire family of channels across the country, using hyperlocal data that changed nightly.

But the *biggest* burden lay upon the shoulders of the research team members who made new presentation slides every single day to support the overnights for all ninety-one Spectrum markets.[8] You can imagine the amount of time and effort this required: new slides every day for every channel in every local market, just so salespeople could approach local businesses.

As complex, difficult, and time-consuming as it was, this is what Spectrum Networks did for years. A constant stream of slides was sent to salespeople out in the field every day to use in their sales presentations. However, there was no real way to conduct analysis on those slides, so the company never really knew which slides were being used by whom, when they were using them, or how effective individual slides were.

That made it practically impossible to tweak and improve slides, so it was a monumental task being performed every day with no system in place for analyzing slide performance.

---

8 "Spectrum Reach operates in 36 states and 91 markets. From reaching millions of households to targeting consumers within 5 miles of your business." Spectrum Reach. https://www.spectrumreach.com/markets-map

Can you imagine if any other form of marketing communication were being done without analysis? Would any company spend millions on a radio or television ad if they had no way to analyze its performance? Yet that was the reality for presentations at Spectrum, just as it continues to be the reality for many companies.

Then Spectrum implemented Presentation Management and created a Structured Storytelling library, and it changed everything. Suddenly, they were able to put out new ratings information quicker and more efficiently by simply updating parent slides with the latest ratings.

At first, they simply applied this to their old method of producing daily slides, but after a few months, they realized they had access to real data about their slides. They could see which slides were being used and by whom, and it gave them insight into which shows on their networks made the greatest emotional impact on clients. Now they could tweak their presentations to make them more effective, honing their messaging and cutting out the dead weight.

Salespeople found that their presentations were more streamlined and effective, which made their jobs a lot easier. The research team that had been preparing those daily slides for ten years had so much menial work taken off their plates that many of them were moved to support other strategic initiatives. In the end, fewer people were needed to update parent slides for the sales team.

Besides making life easier for everyone involved, this represented a tremendous cost savings. Suppose each member of that research team made a salary of $100,000 a year. With five people on the team, the company was spending $500,000 annually on salaries alone to create brand-new slides every day for salespeople in local markets. That adds up to $5,000,000 over ten years. That's a huge amount of money being spent on a tedious task that had no analytics to track the performance of the slides being created—a tedious task that is largely unnecessary with a structured slide library.

In fact, once Spectrum had access to slide data, an analysis of the data revealed that the research team was wasting an inordinate amount of time building content that nobody used. Often, salespeople were making sales without even touching some of the slides that the research department put out, which means a whole lot of work was being done for no practical reason.

Once the company realized this, they were able to stop wasting time on things they didn't need and refocus their efforts on things that had more effect on actual sales. It's just one example of how real scientific data about their presentations through Presentation Management, helped them identify misplaced resources and make their slides more efficient.

MAKING SENSE OF THE DATA

It's one thing to feed someone a bunch of data; it's another thing to make sense of it. The genealogy of slides, as discussed in the previous chapters, helps make sense of the data and gives context to it. Instead of mere quantitative data, you have access to contextualized and qualitative information about each and every slide.

You know the position of the slide within a presentation, how many times it has been viewed, how many times it has been shared with a client, and how much time has been spent on it. You know how many times it has been downloaded, and what your best and worst performers are doing with it.

A structured slide library makes Presentation Management possible by providing a dashboard with easy, succinct information about every slide. First, at the top, you can see the *trends* for any and all activities of all users, files, slides, and shares to give a quick snapshot of what's going on, where slides are going, how many you have, and so on.

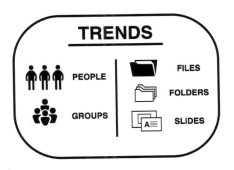

Beneath that, you have two columns that provide more research data. The one on the left shows ***users, groups, and folder permissions***, and the one on the right shows data for ***files and slides***, including the top five files among users. Overlaid on the data, you can see the top slide creators and how many slides were downloaded. Each chart is available as a table, bar chart, line chart, or donut chart, and each one can be downloaded as an image or Excel chart. You can also connect to your API so any of your development teams can send any piece of business intelligence to their senior executives' dashboards.

For example, you could send a chart of the top five files to your CEO's dashboard. That way, the CEO could glance at the corner of their screen and instantly understand which files are in the top five, how they're being used, and how many times they've been presented. All your CEO has to do is click on a file, and they can see exactly how many times it was used and who used it. In other words, every chart becomes a portal to the rest of the data, and every chart can be portaled out to the reporting dashboards of senior executives.

This helps you to identify best practices that you can then instill in other presenters. For example, if your top salesperson always uses a slide that presents a message from the CEO, then maybe you should recommend that other presenters start using that slide. If your worst presenters always just show pricing, then maybe you need to help them build out a story around the prices—or maybe you need to lower your prices.

Consider the popular social media channels of our day. Twitter is a technology that gives you *potential* access to a large audience, but actually reaching that audience depends on how you use the platform. If you want to make a real impact with Twitter, you have to deliver the right message to the right audience in the right way at the right time. The same goes for Facebook. The platform offers the *potential* to create an online community around your company, products, and services, but you have to use it well. Companies that leverage the technology of platforms like Twitter and Facebook wisely reap the rewards in terms of audience engagement.

The same is true of Presentation Management. Presentation Management software is a form of technology that enables companies to communicate with their target audience more effectively, and the medium it uses are presentations. AT&T uses phones, Twitter uses social media posts, and Shufflrr uses slides.

A good piece of Presentation Management software gives you access to a vast array of data about your slides, but making the most of this requires two things: good *reporting* and thorough *analysis*. Reporting refers to the gathering of the data itself—the who, what, when, where, how, and why—and analysis is what you do with that data once you have it.

So, what's the best way to analyze presentation data? Specifically, what's the most important data you can glean from your slides? We recommend the following:

- How many times has it been downloaded?

- How many times has it been used and reused?

- Who has used and reused it?

- How many times has it been viewed by a client?

- How much time was spent on the slide when shared with clients?

If you're not getting *at least* this information from your Presentation Management services, then they are not doing you justice. If you can get even *more* data than this, all the better. Remember, the bigger value equation is how you use that data, but of course, if you don't have access to the data in the first place, then you can't use it.

These five questions give you the basic data you need to identify which slides are most effective, which ones aren't working, and which ones your best and worst presenters rely upon. This, in turn, enables you to hone in on your strengths and prune your weaknesses, which transforms your presentations into a living narrative about your company that keeps getting better over time.

THE MOST IMPORTANT DATA FOR SLIDES

- How many times has it been downloaded?

- How many times has it been used and reused?

- Who used and reused it?

- How many times has it been viewed by client?

- How much time was spent on the slide when shared with clients?

Remember what it was like when you first learned to ride a bicycle? At first, it was tough, and you kept wobbling, losing your balance, and falling. Maybe you skinned your knees a couple of times. Over time, however, as you practiced and built up momentum, you found that you could maintain your balance and control of the bicycle with greater ease. It didn't take long until you could ride a bike with such ease that you hardly had to think about it.

The same goes with Presentation Management. As the data comes in, the pieces are going to begin falling into place. You'll start figuring out what works and what doesn't, and you'll be able to lean more into your strengths. Once you're flying fast and confidently, your communications will be constantly up to date, relevant, and telling the same compelling story about your company. You will be able to anticipate the slides you need to reinforce product launches.

Never again will you have to start from scratch when you want to give a presentation because your presentation communication channel will provide a steady stream of data that allows you to anticipate changes, adjust on the fly, and share the best and most impactful stories with every presentation. Everyone will always be using the right logos, the right colors, the right messages, and the right language. Information will always be correct and current, and there will be no more gaps in your knowledge about who is doing what.

Do you see how dramatically this is going to change the way you present? In some ways, we're only just now realizing the impact of Presentation Management on the way we present, sell, and communicate. Let's take a glimpse into the near future to see what Structured Storytelling might look like very soon.

CHAPTER 12

A PRESENTATION STRATEGY FOR GOING FORWARD

YOU'RE STANDING ON STAGE AT CARNEGIE HALL, ABOUT to give a presentation to a packed house. All of your slides containing all of your documents are hovering like holograms in the air beside you—just offstage where only you can see them. There are slides with videos, with photos, with art, graphs, documents—all sorts of things.

As you speak, you reach out and swipe one of the hologram images with your right hand, and suddenly it appears on a big screen behind you in super high resolution. Then you swipe another slide and Beethoven's Ninth Symphony starts to play, booming out over the audience. You swipe up, and a 3D graphic appears, animated to the music. You're like a conductor of a symphony orchestra, but your instruments are your files.

All of these files are coming from your slide library, and they include a full range of multimedia content. You're able to create a live digital production of such quality that it's like you're producing a movie right then and there before your audience.

That's the near future of presentations, and you might even see it today. You won't have to be at Carnegie Hall to have access to it. Indeed, soon the average Joe or Jane on the street will be able to turn around and pull up any multimedia content in their library right there. Any video, any image, any document can be pulled out of their library at a moment's notice and played live, as if it were a musical instrument in the hands of a trained artist.

Imagine a world where Presentation Management is managing all of your content at all times and making it accessible and available to you, ready to present. We've used the metaphor of your smartphone's photo library, but what we're moving toward is even more robust and powerful than pulling up organized photos on your phone.

A LIVING, BREATHING SYSTEM OF COMMUNICATION

Presentation management is already being used in some creative and surprising ways by global companies, including one we've already mentioned: Medline Industries. We recently designed a feature in our Shufflrr software that enables users to save their files as videos instead of presentation slides. Medline is using this feature to create videos that they can use to train critical care specialists and clinicians on using their products whenever they make a purchase. These videos work as both sales tools *and* training tools, both before and after a sale, and they can be played separately or integrated seamlessly alongside all of their other slides.

Medline's slide library, this living, breathing system of communication, is actually serving different groups within Medline with very different needs. On the one hand, they are creating traditional sales presentations about Medline products that reps can use to make pitches. On the other hand, they are also creating product portfolios for customers that contain custom training docs and training videos for the products they've purchased. Furthermore, training content contains very specific instructions to teach nurses, doctors, and healthcare providers how to use Medline products safely and effectively, to help rather than harm patients.

Good Presentation Management is able to handle all of these different needs simultaneously, while still keeping every presentation on message and on brand at all times. It's like a conductor swinging their baton to keep a complex array of musicians and instruments playing together in rhythm and harmony: every instrument playing its own part in sync with every other instrument to create a single piece of beautiful music.

And that's just one example of the many new and creative ways that business leaders are using Presentation Management to change the way they do business. It's not just about how you use your presentations, it's also about getting the most out of the robust data that's available on slide use. Imagine how it's going to change your approach to presentations when you can see how many times people have viewed each slide, how they've used it, and what their reaction was.

This kind of data will enable you to curate your slide library, eliminating the dead weight that's not doing you any good, bolstering the content that is effective, and improving the nuances that seem to generate the strongest positive response. A process of constant improvement like this is going to make your messaging tighter, stronger, and more consistent throughout your organization.

In that way, it's similar to other forms of communication. If Budweiser runs a Super Bowl ad that gets a huge positive response and results in a surge in sales, they're going to run that ad again many times. They might even create a whole ad campaign that plays off the same themes to keep the momentum going. Now, you can do the same thing with your presentations. You're treating them just like any other form of marketing or sales communication, leaning into what works and making your message more effective over time.

Analytics ensures that each slide becomes iterative, constantly tweaked and improved by your content admins, and if the data shows that a slide doesn't work, as we said, it can be cut entirely. You're managing a global communication tool that affects the verbiage being used across your entire organization, and as you make it better and better, you make your entire organization better and better at communicating the value of what you have to offer.

At the same time, because you're treating each presentation like a story, and every slide like a scene, you're going to be making a deeper and more emotional impact on your audience. Think about it: every person in your entire organization getting better and more consistent at telling impactful stories about your products and services, and they're always on message, on brand, with relevant and accurate information at all times in every presentation everywhere.

No other communication channel has the potential to make such a profound impact on every person in your entire global organization. Every slide and every presentation will be right at your fingertips, always up to date and constantly getting better, giving you immediate access so you can use, reuse, and repurpose any of your content instantly. What an incredible resource for communicating your value, answering questions and concerns, and spreading the story of your brand far and wide. It makes every person a more effective and intelligent storyteller.

When you have data that shows what people look at and how they respond, you can help clients make informed decisions backed with real data. It's a living, breathing system, and it's poised to change the world. In fact, the change is already here. We're talking about interactive presentations that enable you to present spontaneously to clients. No need to prepare a dry speech or practice it repeatedly in front of the mirror or to your spouse or roommate. The slide library is going to give you everything you need.

Imagine if everyone at a meeting had your presentation on their phones, and as soon as they asked a question, AI picked up the words from their phone and instantly suggested the right slides to the presenter so they could respond to the question. Imagine if your Presentation Management software curated questions from a large audience, selected the most important ones, *and* suggested the most appropriate response?

This level of interactivity is just around the corner. The days of awkward, cobbled-together, linear presentations that can't follow your audience, can't respond to their questions and concerns, and provide conflicting messages are over.

No more getting dumped by PowerPoint. And no more presentation hell. Now, every person in the company is telling stories, sharing impactful and consistent messages across your organization using all of your best content, responding to your audience in the moment, and making a deeper and more compelling emotional impact backed by data that leads clients to a decision far more naturally and effectively.

That is Presentation Management, and it's the future of presentations: better stories, with the best content, all backed by data. And you can get a head start on that future right now.

CONCLUSION

TELLING BETTER STORIES

YOU CAN TELL BETTER STORIES THAT RESONATE WITH YOUR audience, and when you resonate with your audience, they are more likely to buy, act, or respond as you intended. More than that, if you tell a really powerful story, they are going to retell it, which makes it viral.

You've seen this virality at work in other communication channels. When that funny ad runs during the Super Bowl, there are people discussing it the next day, retelling it and reenacting it for weeks, months, years to come. Heck, you probably still know at least one person who says, "Whaz-zup!" And that Super Bowl ad ran way back in 1999. Those kinds of viral ads become fodder for other media, including references in sitcoms, social media posts, and funny TikTok videos. They get talked about in the break room at work. They become an inspiration for in-jokes that family and friends tell at get-togethers. They might even inspire other ads from other companies.

Storytelling has always been this way. Stories are passed down from generation to generation. The really good ones inspire other stories. Important details from those stories get woven deeply into cultures and even the ordinary experiences of everyday people. Indeed, people are eager to tell and retell the best stories because they know the audience is going to react.

It's the reason we discuss popular movies. It's the reason fans of certain TV shows, movies, and books have elaborate conventions where they can continue to discuss their favorite stories and find creative ways to interact with them for years to come.

That same sort of virality can happen with your presentations. The stories you tell in your presentations can get retold and reshared, inspiring other stories, long after the audience first heard them. From a business standpoint, if you give a presentation to one client, and they can effectively retell your story to their colleagues, it's going to have a far more profound impact than if you share the story with each of them yourself.

Viral stories make your job a whole lot easier, and storytelling drives virality more than anything else. Indeed, the best stories are designed to be easy to understand and easy to retell. They make an immediate emotional impact and have a clear plot that leads to a poignant, moving, or amusing conclusion.

With Structured Storytelling, you're organizing all of your content so that it's formatted to present, published in a slide library, but just as important, you're weighing the emotional impact of every slide. Every presentation tells a story, and every slide is a scene. Data and dry information are couched in impactful stories designed with intentionality.

Yesterday's presentations were preordained, linear slideshows that were often hastily constructed from a tangled mess of slides. They weren't often intended to tell stories or evoke specific emotions, nor could presenters readily respond and react to the audience. Instead, the presenter was usually trying to shove an audience down a predetermined path no matter how they felt, reacted, or responded, with little ability to adjust on the fly.

Now you're like the old storyteller sitting around the campfire, telling your most profound tales to a captivated audience, but you're also following their emotional journey, able to react and bolster your story by answering questions and leaning into the emotion.

SCRATCHING THE SURFACE

What does the future look like? Every single person in your organization is able to present as effectively as the CEO. Your entire global organization continually gets better, giving more consistent and impactful presentations every day.

It all begins when you start bringing some order to the tangled mess of slides that are scattered in folders all across your organization and beyond. Create your slide library, organize all of your content, trim the fat, format everything to present, impose some intentionality on every slide, and create your structured slide library.

Of course, you can do all of this yourself. It may seem like a big task, but cleaning a cluttered house is hard work, too. And it's a big task that can be tackled efficiently with the processes we've given you. All of that work is worth it in the end. The benefits of creating your own structured slide library will be worth whatever it takes to get there.

However, the whole process becomes a lot easier when you invest in good Presentation Management software. The choice is yours, but we strongly recommend you get started right away. If you're still using the old cobbled-together mess of linear presentations, you're in Presentation Hell.

You're missing out on the real power of Structured Story-telling and Presentation Management.

Imagine: a whole channel of communication available to your organization, and you've only scratched the surface of its potential!

WE'RE READY TO HELP

For additional help, advice, and resources on Presentation Management, check out our website at www.Shufflrr.com. There, you will find information about Shufflrr, our robust Presentation Management system and communication strategy hub for enterprise. Shufflrr keeps your messaging, branding, images, data, and more synchronized throughout your business's presentation library, so content is easier to find, easier to reuse, and easier to track. It's the easiest and most powerful way to implement Structured Storytelling and Presentation Management throughout your organization.

"Shufflrr cuts time creating new presentations from five hours to five minutes."

—US Bank

GLOSSARY OF TERMS

Chain of custody - Data verification of the journey of a slide, revealing who created it, who approved it, who moved it to the next step in the presentation workflow, who has used it, who has shared it, who has viewed it, and more.

Compliance - There are two primary types of compliance. *Brand* compliance refers to consistency in the look and feel of graphics, fonts, and logos as well as the rules and codes of conduct that a business implements internally to ensure high operating standards. *Regulatory/ legal* compliance refers to the rules and regulations set by regulatory government agencies that a company must adhere to, mostly in regard to approved verbiage (e.g., proper disclosures).

Ben Franklin - A statesman, author, inventor, kite-flyer, and Founding Father of the United States of America who lived from 1706 to 1790. Coined many famous sayings and catchphrases, including, "A place for everything, everything in its place."

Corporate slide library - A shared slide library in which every slide is formatted to present, then published and presented as a "Structured Story" similar to a table of contents. A corporate slide library contains all of a company's individual slides for every issue, ensuring that every slide used by anyone in the organization is easy to find, up to date, compliant, and tells the same overarching brand story.

David Ogilvy - A British advertising tycoon and the Founder of Ogilvy & Mather, known as the "Father of Advertising."

Elay Cohen - The CEO and Co-founder of SalesHood (a leading sales enablement platform) and author of the books *Enablement Mastery* and *SalesHood*.

Genealogy of a slide - The DNA of communication through a slide, revealing every instance that it was used, shared, downloaded and reused, as well as who used it.

Glossophobia - (glos·so·pho·bia) *noun* - Fear of public speaking.

Hoarders - American reality television series on A&E that depicts the real-life struggles and treatment of people who suffer from compulsive hoarding disorder. Similarly, "slide hoarders" are people who gather and keep all of their slides, whether they are up to date and useful or not.

Marc Benioff - The Co-founder, Chairman, and Co-CEO of Salesforce, an enterprise cloud computing company that was also the first SaaS business.

Nancy Duarte - A writer, speaker, expert in presentation design, and CEO of Duarte Design.

Parent–child relationship - The relationship between the original published slide (parent) and a duplicate (child) that is reused in a new presentation. In a Structured Story, that relationship is linked and tracked, which yields data that reveals the genealogy of a slide.

Pitchman[9] - Multimedia presentation software that was the foundation for iXL in the late 1990s. In 2000, James spun out Pitchman to create a new company, Iguana Interactive.

Presentation event - Which presentation was used (presentation ID)

- Who presented it (user ID)

- When this event occurred (time stamp)

- Mode of the event (online, in person)

- Event type (sales pitch, employee orientation, etc.)

---

9 "First Union Elects Bert Ellis to Board." *Atlanta Business Chronicle,* https://www.bizjournals.com/atlanta/stories/1997/06/09/daily8.html

- Audience profile

- Company defined

Presentation life cycle - All of the stages of a slide through its various iterations and revisions: creation, distribution, presentation, sharing, feedback, reporting, and updating.

Presentation Management - An enterprise strategy for managing all of your communications through presentations, which includes the life cycle of all slides.

SlideCart™ - The temporary storage area where you place your slides and reorder them before saving a new presentation. It's similar to an internet shopping cart, but it's filled with slides instead of products.

Structured Storytelling - Similar to a table of contents, Structured Storytelling is the organization of folders, files, and slides into an organized, published library that enables every single team member to communicate the value of the company, products, and services. Presentations are organized as chapters, and individual slides are the scenes in those chapters. If you have good Structured Storytelling, you have a winning strategy for Presentation Management.

Tangled mess of slides - When slides are everywhere throughout your network: on hard drives, in network folders, work sites, and individual emails. There's no central location where slides are systematically stored, tagged, and updated so anyone can easily find and reuse the right version of each slide. Today, most corporations operate this way. This is often the result of "slide hoarding."

Wild West approach - When everyone is doing their own thing with slides throughout the organization, so you get wildly different verbiage, text, and graphics, without consistency.

ACKNOWLEDGMENTS

We'd like to thank April, Buddy, Susan, Joey, Kyle, and Dylan. Your love and support help us every day. And, special thanks to Embarc Collective, Tampa.

We wish to express our gratitude to all of the client companies we've worked with over the years. Thanks for trusting us to help prepare, improve, and manage your presentations.

That list includes a wide variety of clients in a wide array of industries:

INFORMATION TECHNOLOGY

Apple, Cisco, Dell, Splunk, VMware

HEALTHCARE

Cigna, Covance, Genentech, LabCorp, Medline, McKesson, NIH, Novartis, Pfizer, Roche, Teva Pharmaceuticals, Takeda Pharmaceuticals

FINANCIALS

ADP, American Express, Bloomberg, Comerica, US Bank

CONSUMER DISCRETIONARY

British Airways, Choice Hotels, DHL, Hertz, Hilton, IHG, James Bond, John Deere, Kodak, Kelly Services, LEGO, Loews Hotels, Mercedes-Benz, NBA, NFL, Olympics, Royal Caribbean Group

COMMUNICATION SERVICES

ABC, Alliance Atlantis, AOL, AT&T, BET, CBS, Charter, Comedy Central, Discover, Disney, Epcot Center, ESPN, Food Network, FOX, HGTV, NBC, New York City Commission for Human Rights, Nielsen, Paramount, Screenvision, Sirius Satellite Radio, Telemundo, Time Warner Cable, TransPerfect, Tribune, Warner Bros., Weather Channel, Showtime, Verizon

INDUSTRIALS

GE, NASA

CONSUMER STAPLES

Keurig, Starbucks

ENERGY

HESS, Schlumberger

MATERIALS

De Beers

ABOUT THE AUTHORS

JAMES ONTRA AND ALEXANNDRA ONTRA are a brother-sister team who have worked together since 2000, developing and marketing Presentation Management software. They founded their own company, Ontra Presentations, in 2002 with a borrowed desk, two phones, and licensing rights to the Iguana Presentation system, which James swapped his employment contract to obtain. James and AlexAnndra cold-called prospects every day for eight hours a day, and within ninety days had landed ABC National Television Stations and Towers Perrin. Twenty years, seven different software applications (some discontinued, some still going) and over a hundred Fortune-level clients later, both are still developing Presentation Management solutions that help their clients share, shuffle and show their content.

While the technology has certainly changed over the years, and Shufflrr is the latest iteration, the market and the need are still the same: business-to-business sales and training teams who need a fast, simple way to create, give, and share presentations, all while ensuring brand and message compliance.

PRAISE

"With Ontra technology, we can access our entire portfolio of products anywhere, anytime. Its flexibility and adaptability make it easy to customize our presentations on a dime."

—**Cathy Egan,** SVP, ABC National Television Sales

"(With Ontra) we now have a presentation platform that matches the quality programming and audience that the NBC television stations deliver."

—**Mike Chico,** Executive Vice President, NBCUniversal Television Stations Sales

"Our Ontra presentation is great. We used it from day one and signed up fifty new subscribers at our first trade show."

—**Steven Faigen,** Chief Marketing Officer, Global Talent at Towers Perrin

"In keeping with the FOX tradition of producing distinctive, original entertainment, we were searching for a presentation solution that would engage and entertain our audience while delivering the facts of our story. Ontra Presentation software allows us to present our information in a more dynamic and attention-grabbing way."

—**Audrey Steele,** EVP Sales Research
Insight & Strategy at FOX Corp.

"When we set out to buy some new presentation software, we considered a number of products that seemed similar. After interviewing current customers for each product, we finally chose Ontra. Ontra got rave reviews for being a customer-centric small business... and it was true. Not only did our presentation look great (so good that now other groups in our company are considering upgrading to Ontra) but everyone at Ontra, from the founders to the designers, were available to us for all of our quick-turnaround needs."

—**Sandra Szahun,** Warner Bros., Director,
Integrated Sales & Marketing

"For years I have been looking for a way to make our programming grids interactive to showcase our vast array of offerings. Finally, technology has caught up to our needs through the Ontra software. The Ontra

organization was pleasant and professional to deal with every step of the way through the process."

—**Brad Alles,** SVP Broadcast Sales, Alliance Atlantis

"With Ontra's 3D Theater, everyone gets it! Advertisers understand how their brand will look within the theater. And sales executives have an easier time selling it through."

—**Todd Siegel,** EVP Sales, Screen Vision

"Ontra Presentation software allows us to create incredibly dynamic presentations that are easy for our development officers to use. We have certainly set ourselves apart from the pack."

—**Catherine Camera,** St. John's University, Associate Vice President for Alumni Relations and Development

"The Ontra Presentation allows all of our salespeople to speak intelligently whether talking about the details of one program or the value of working with Scripps in general. With the Ontra Presentation, they can now cross-sell the networks, which translates into higher revenues for all of Scripps."

—**Jon Steinlauf,** Chief US Advertising Sales Officer, Warner Bros Discovery

James and Alex are thought leaders in presentations and storytelling. Presentation Hell *is a must-read for all executives looking to uplevel their stakeholder communications.*

—**Elay Cohen,** CEO & Co-Founder of SalesHood, and author of the books *Enablement Mastery* and *SalesHood*

BOOK DESCRIPTION

"Invest in yourself. The one easy way to become worth 50 percent more is to hone your communication skills—both written and verbal. You can have all the brainpower in the world, but you have to be able to transmit it."

—**Warren Buffett**

PUBLIC SPEAKING AND SLIDE PRESENTATIONS ARE AN enduring combination. But just because PowerPoint has become standard practice doesn't mean you're using it in the most impactful way.

Your company has a story to share. What if each slide in your presentation was a scene in this story? What if your messaging was consistently compelling and enabled you to interact with your audience and guarantee a connection? In *Presentation Hell,* Shufflrr founders James Ontra and

AlexAnndra Ontra reveal how your company can transform the entire presentation experience from tedious and painful to dynamic and rewarding. Their proprietary systems for Structured Storytelling and Presentation Management streamline preparation by providing an organized slide library of polished slides with consistent language. You'll learn how to facilitate better conversations, respond impactfully in critical moments, and reinforce messaging in every step. Featuring revolutionary strategies that apply to every industry, *Presentation Hell* is today's bible for making your communication count.

PRESENTATION

Podcast

Spotify • Apple Podcasts • iHeart Radio •
Amazon • Audible • PlayerFM • Google Podcasts
• ListenNotes • PocketCasts

Presentation Strategies That Work

Presentation Management and Structured Storytelling

Get out of Presentation Hell

START YOUR STRUCTURED STORY